SHE WANTED MORE

A story of pain, strength, revival and victory

SPARKLE CHRISTINE

She Wanted More Copyright © 2019 by Sparkle C. Buntyon.

All rights reserved. Printed in the United States of America. No part of this book may be used or reproduced in any manner whatsoever without written permission except in the case of brief quotations em- bodied in critical articles or reviews.

Scriptures taken from the New International Version (NIV) Bible.

Photography by Michelle Morrow (Lord Morrow Photography)

For information contact www.sophisticateddreemz.com

ISBN: 978-1-7342618-0-6

First Edition: November 2019

CONTENTS

Contents

Introduction 1

Early Years 4

Losing My Way 18

Adulting Times Two 29

Learning the Strongholds 39

The Girl in the Mirror 50

Ministry? I Think Not 61

Manifesting the Dreemz 72

Journaling Through the Dreemz 81

About the Author 86

Acknowledgments 88

INTRODUCTION

Philippians 4:11-13

"I am not saying this because I am in need, for I have learned to be content whatever the circumstances. I know what it is to be in need, and I know what it is to have plenty. I have learned the secret of being content in any and every situation, whether well fed or hungry, whether living in plenty or in want. I can do everything through him who gives me strength."

YOU ARE INVITED TO WATCH AS A YOUNG GIRL AWAKENS to a world of missed opportunity, struggle, and pain. Born in Indianapolis, Indiana in the mid 80's to a soft-hearted mother, and a father who believed only the strong would survive, I was to be whisked away to the musical city of Memphis, TN where the story begins. In the transitionto Memphis my parents would separate, and I would not meet my father until 2006 when I moved to Minneapolis, MN. There is much detail regarding that transition, however, that is not my story to tell.

Sparkle Christine

Throughout my childhood, I would have to settle with hushed mentions of what my father was like from my big brother as we huddled in fear of my stepfather. The unfinished business of wanting to know who my father was chased me like a shadow throughout my life. Although I had the opportunity to meet my father when I moved to Minneapolis and spend four years in the same city with him as an adult, the damage created in my formative years was as present and painful as a fresh bruise.

I would shuffle through my youth embittered by poverty, trauma, bullying and small glimpses of a God that I wasn't sure loved me. It led me through a web of bad decisions: drugs, sex and, consequently, a teen mother. And, much like my father, I believed only the strong survive. My earliest memories involve my refusal to allow myself to admit defeat, to admit that I was hurting, and that I was a powerless victim of circumstance. I created this tough exterior to mask the enervated shell of myself with determination and self-motivation to save me from the only world I knew. I just knew that I had it all together. I felt that if I could control everything then nothing could ever again control me. This determination alone allowed me to finish high school; and thereafter, a post vocational school where I obtained my Associate in Applied Science degree in Business.

As I write this now, I laugh. I laugh because it was that tenacity that ultimately led me to Christ. The God I was introduced to in my childhood taught me to fear him, in a most uncomfortable way. It was not until I made him real to me in my late twenties, that I was able to understand God's other qualities that kept me throughout my life. The characteristics of grace, mercy and love. It was this love that pushed me to healing and forgiveness. It is that same love that drives me to write this book as a full circle moment to my life of excruciating inner pain and turmoil. It is that love that invites you into my heart and my life, hoping to impact you in such a way that you feel the very love of Jesus. In writing this, I hope to reach the person who has travelled a painful

SHE WANTED MORE

road but may not yet understand why. My friend, this is what I leave you with: there is always a purpose for your pain.

When I initially thought to pen my life, I was intensely aware of the stigma involved in telling one's story amongst People of Color. That very stigma stopped me from vocalizing my intentions to friends and family for nearly a decade, however, there is something to be said for the natural progression of the seasons: winter to spring, spring to summer and summer to fall. There is an evolvement that must take place before changes can occur. Such was my leap into taking the route of faith and strength I knew would be needed to write this book. It was these changes, or "Growth Work" as I like to call it that allowed me to walk into grace. Grace, otherwise known as a second chance. This story, my story, is still being written. However, I welcome you to glance into my journey, where it began and where I am today. This is where God revealed the purpose in my pain.

Welcome to my Second Act!

1

Early Years

MY EARLIEST MEMORIES AS A CHILD ARE OF ME AND MY OLDER BROTHER STEPHEN PLAYING IN OUR HOUSE IN MEMPHIS. My mother would later tell me that we were a troublesome pair, always getting into things and creating a stir. While my oldest brother Christopher could be found doing some task that did not cause commotion, Stephen and I found happiness in anything that could be considered loud and rambunctious. My days were filled with playing hide and go seek, trying out new words we learned as we listened in on my mother's conversations with her friends, and fearfully running from the mice we shared the home with that came out to play. My nights were very different. Even as I write this, I get faint feelings of heartache because nights in our home were filled with anxiety and uncertainty when my stepfather would come home from working. I don't remember him being there very long in the evenings, but the time he was home, before heading out to his nightly visits to the casino, were long, drawn out and traumatic. I didn't know it at the time, but I would later learn that it was during these times that I would begin to develop a

She Wanted more

fear of men that would follow me into adulthood.

My stepfather was a direct, no nonsense kind of man. He packed a forceful blow of abrasive words with a voice that could make you faint if directed towards you. We often felt both of his attentions were on us. I am still uncertain, today, of what caused his anger with life or with us as kids. I think I would have asked him if I had enough nerve. Still, that question is one I would never voice. I learned quickly to avoid him at all costs as the ruling philosophy of our house at the sound of his footsteps was that children were to be seen and not heard. Alas, there was much to see during that time. Mostly, I would see him leave very early in the morning and come back around dinner time. He would have the same routine for nearly twenty years.

Every day, at the same time the house would begin its descent from carefree lighthearted fun, into tension and a quiet nervousness I could not identify until much later in my youth. Looking back, I am imagining that my mother may have felt the same anxiousness. Even as a small girl, I would notice how she would frantically take his call in the afternoon as he alerted her that he would be on his way home. She would shush us into a quiet place and make sure we did not have anything out of place that might upset him. Mother would hurriedly prepare his bath so it would be hot and welcoming when he arrived. Even then, I could sense her working very hard to please him. It was almost as if she wanted him to acknowledge and praise her for how she had his bath ready, and a meal prepared.

When he would finally walk in the door, he would speak to us kids and disappear to his bath and then their bedroom. My mother would join him. I don't remember when I learned to not disturb them or need my mother when my stepfather was home. It may have been an unexplained rule. In the event we would need to knock on the door to ask a question, or need our mother, there would be prompt thrashing of obscenities. Accordingly, that little ball of fear I learned to live with so

Sparkle Christine

well would begin to rise. My mother would do her best to prep me before he came home. She would say things like, "Remember when he gets home not to knock on the door. It was their time to have together and talk." I would always wonder why that time could not occasionally include the four of us siblings who were left in the bedroom or the living room to entertain each other until she could resurface when he left home for the night. After she would have completed the routine each day, he and his fondness for alcohol would still leave us for his first love, the casino or the racetrack, whichever tickled his fancy most for the night. These were my earliest memories of feeling abandoned. When I reflect on these times, I believe my mother felt abandoned too. My heart still burns for the young woman that was my mother during those years, yearning for attention from her husband, while struggling to provide emotional support to her children that she did not have to give.

Growing up, there was usually some uncertainty over where we would live, and at times what we would eat as my parents weren't the greatest managers of money. For several years we would only be in one place for short periods of time. We saw them both go to work every day and work hard they did, but not save money or teach us financial stability. That is something that carried on to the four of us kids. However, we not only learned how to work, but to work hard. I am eternally grateful for them teaching us that. That great work ethic is something I would need to carry me through the rest of my life. Sadly, that hard work rarely translated into stability inside the home. They did the best with the knowledge they had at the time, and with the demons of their own childhood.

I remember summers when I wanted to help my mom out with the cooking to alleviate some of her stress with working and trying to make sure we had enough food and other essentials. My stepfather was there physically but provided little support to my mom, so I wanted lighten her load as much as possible. I would cook meals and share meal plans that I had created with her using the sparse amount of food we had to

SHE WANTED MORE

work with. I always thought doing this would help calm her, so in my desire to please her, I would use the meal plans to cook for everyone so we could stretch the little food we had. I am not sure if it helped much, but I tried. I know she loved us, and I wanted her to know I loved her enough to try and ease her burden of taking care of us kids. Mom wasn't very vocal with telling us she loved us. She tried to show it in other ways, by working hard to give us what we needed, and a little of what we wanted when able. Saying the words never came easy for her. I don't vividly remember her telling me that she loved me until I was about thirteen years old. Until that time, I only felt in the way as I grew up in the era of children were to be heard and not seen.

Love has always been an interesting concept to me. What was it exactly? How was it shown? Is it pain or are there good things associated with it? Although, the only father I knew as a child was angry and mean spirited most days, I loved him and still do today. Reminiscing on my childhood, there were brief moments where I remember my stepfather smiling or playing with me. Still, as a child, I felt mostly fear and anxiety with him being there. Looking back upon those times now as an adult, I believe he loved me and my siblings as much as he could considering the inner emotional turmoil he dealt with.

Today, many people use the aphorism, "hurt people, hurt people" when referencing emotional pain. I am not sure of where the saying originated, yet it reigns as a true statement in my opinion. It is one that I would spend most of my life trying to decipher, with myself being the primary subject. I didn't know much about what love was or what caused people to hurt when I was just a little kid trying to learn what the world was all about. I do know I desperately felt a need to be loved and protected. There was much uncertainty on what the days would bring, but in my heart, I knew through the ball of tension in my gut that safety and love were not there. I heard stories as I got older of what my stepfather had been like as a boy. In his youth, his father, a hard man such as himself, died leaving his mother to care for a handful of

Sparkle Christine

children. I assumed this heavily weighed on him and impacted how he responded to life after that. I wanted to know more about him, so I would ask questions as the opportunities arose. My stepfather played football and was what they call a man's man. It was a slow process, but during the few times I hung around his family, I learned things about the man that remained a mystery to me much of my young life. I learned that he loved and lost, and that might just be why he was unable to shake off whatever was chasing him in his dreams from youth.

Out of my four immediate siblings, I was the only child to challenge him. Now, I knew limits, especially since he didn't mind raising a hand along with his voice. But, to this day my mother says that he loved me the hardest because I would tell him what I thought. I always felt as though she said this proudly, but in my mind, I wondered why that was a statement of pride instead of discontent. I would rather someone share their thoughts with me because they felt a trust or a bond, certainly not out of anger for how one was being treated. I knew even then the feelings of injustice and how that made me feel. I was a defender of the fragile spirit mom inhibited, and of the resentment my brothers carried. There were many times when I would beg my mother to leave him with the naïve view of life as a child. It would all be simple. My mother would just pack us all in her station wagon, drive us to an undisclosed location where we would all magically be happy, and life would start anew. Problem solved, right? As most of us learn as we progress in age, life does not happen that way. It certainly didn't happen that way for us. There are these things that come along commonly known as bumps in the road, or challenges. For my mother, I later learned the challenges were the stumbling blocks that would cause her to still be with him today, as I write this book. As I reflect, I was the tough one. Even today, I like a good challenge. I always thought of myself as the lone ranger responsible for defending anyone who could not stand up for themselves against the bullies of the world. But the task involved in defending the treatment of my mother and my brothers to my

She Wanted more

stepfather, was one that caused great physical and emotional pain.

When I was pregnant with my daughter, my family and I were undergoing major life changes associated with our living arrangements. One night, during an unsuccessful attempt at sleep, I was awakened by loud voices. I recognized the voices as my mom and stepfather. They were returning from an all too often trip to the casino. As usual, my stepfather had too much to drink and was drunk. I opened the door and saw her attempting to usher him down the hall to their bedroom. The sight of him yelling at my mother and being completely drunken and unruly incinerated me. We were accustomed to the sight of both, him yelling at her, her taking it in silence, and him being drunk out of all reality. I can still smell the beer on his breath today. All 5'4" of me stepped into the hallway, stared the drunken beast down and said, "Why do you have to talk to her like that? You are wrong for speaking to her that way, and it's disgusting that you are drunk." Well, my stepfather was never one to back down from a fight, and for that matter neither was I. Regardless of blood ties, I still emulated some of his mannerisms, etc. If I learned and imitated anything from my stepfather, it was his stubborn spirit. Here we were, standing defender to oppressor ready to battle. He turns to me, says his usual threatening words as my mother tries to get me to back down and retreat, and he continues saying words I will take with me to my grave. In a cold drunken voice, he says, "I don't care if I whoop her ass, she is my wife, there is not a damn thing you can do about it." In that moment, I am sure you are guessing I came back at him with something much tougher, harsher and full of energy. His few words spoken had a smaller effect on me. The man I knew had spoken much worse words over the course of sixteen years. The immediate sense of defeat I felt and saw, in my mother, as the man she gave her life away to uncaringly mouthed those chilling words, shattered me. She vocalized not one word, but the cry of hurt and sadness in her eyes was deafening at the realization of what her years of service, submission and loveall summed up to in those few callouswords

Sparkle Christine

spoken by this broken man. So, what did I do? Well, I watched him turn and say, "Come on Kris," that is what he called her. She meekly followed him to the room, and they shut the door. I sadly went back into my room and cried myself to sleep.

Very vividly, I remember hoping, as I often had to growing up, that he did not hurt my mother when I couldn't be in the bedroom to defend her. I thought this because I knew that she would not defend herself. Conversely, I enjoyed the occasional carefree moments my siblings and I spent with my stepfather at his favorite places to eat like Church's Chicken and McDonald's. I quickly learned I was his favorite and his adversary. The result was mixed feelings of love and anger towards a man I desperately wanted to understand. I wondered how he grew up. Was my upbringing with him similar? Maybe he just gave us love the only way he knew how. I would have to become content with never knowing the answer but loving him despite it all.

What is more, I was struggling with him and thoughts of who my real father was. I remember a time when I thought my mom's husband was my one and only father. One night, many years ago when I was very young, my brother Stephen told me a hurtful truth. He told me that my stepfather wasn't my dad. Up to that point, I had always called him daddy. After that, I never did again. He became Lawrence. I know that hurt him. Even today, I can feel sympathy for the pain he must have felt in hearing me say those words to him. But I felt pain, too. I felt pain and confusion that still has not been explained to me to this day. My mother never told me the story of why she kept it from me. Again, it was one of those things we would not speak of. Stephen and I share the same father. I later learned that my mother and father were both from Indianapolis, Indiana. My brother told me tales of them fighting, that my mother later confirmed. I later learned that my father was abusive to my mother, and she left him. Two months after I was born, she met my stepfather and they have been married since. Over the years, I would ask about my father to no avail. My mother would not speak ill of him,

She Wanted more

but she would not tell me about who he was either. When I was a teenager, I found his brother on the internet. The need to understand him haunted me into action. I contacted him, and he put me in touch with my father. Steve Hollins was a rolling stone. I learned that he had at least seven other children outside of my brother and myself. He was in Minnesota at the time but had lived for a time in Indiana. I remember our first conversation and the mixed feelings that ensued. He'd promise to come and get me so I could live with him. He would save me from the only home I'd known. I waited and waited. He never showed up. I am still not sure I can describe the pain felt. I won't even try. It was just another notch in my lack-of-trust-belt. Even with that, in 2006 I moved myself and Tiana, my daughter, to Minneapolis to better know him. In the four and a half years I spent there, I would only see my father a total of five times. I am grateful for the memory of him attending my wedding to my first husband, while my stepfather walked me down the aisle. He showed up. For the moment in time, I felt loved by him. It was an important day in my life, and he showed up. He died in 2012 from cancer. I hurt for the man I wished I'd known more about, and for the little girl who only wanted her father to love her.

Although we had family up in Indianapolis, much of our family lived close by us in Memphis. For whatever reason, my parents did not allow close relationships with our cousins, aunts and uncles. We were always isolated and contained to the house when they were out, or the front and backyard of our home when my mom was home. If my parents were away from home, they locked their door where the telephone was. There we sat, with no telephone, a TV and each other to keep company. It was lonely and what I believe drove me into the world of books. When I read, I could step away from the loneliness and sadness I felt in being kept away from the world. Now friends, keep in mind that I was the vocal one in the group, raging against all injustices. In response, my mother would tell me she wanted to protect us, and we would understand when we got older. Looking back, I can agree that I now

Sparkle Christine

understand her point of view. Even so, I agree that her will to protect us was damaging in a lot of ways to our development and ability to relate to others as we grew into adults. Furthermore, being a mother myself, has allowed me to understand more about my own mother as a woman and to compassionately connect with where she was and how she got to the place to where she wanted to protect us. Moving along, there were times when my grandparents visited, and the entire family would gather for barbeques at one of our family homes in town. It was then that we were able to visit with our cousins and try to bond. Those visits never went well for me. I have to say, there is only one cousin out of the multiplicity of cousins I have that I was able to form a bond with. Unfortunately, that did not happen until we became women many years later. I love her deeply and am grateful for a second chance to get to know her. Back then I felt anxious and awkward amongst my cousins, not knowing or understanding the games they played, dances danced or things they talked about. I wanted to be accepted, but I quickly learned how little I knew about how to interact with girls my own age. I had brothers and one stepsister who I did not get to see much except in the summertime and it wasn't because my stepfather and her mother weren't fighting.

Even though my mother was trying to figure out life for herself with four kids, she still tried to find ways to love us the only ways she knew how. I have memories of her picking me up from school early. On those days, we would go to her favorite Chinese buffet and eat together. It was our time for me to feel special.It is a good memory that we share.What's funny is that I would find out later in life that she did the same thing with my siblings too.Similarly, she would pack us all up to board a bus heading to Lamberts Café in Missouri. This restaurant was famous for throwing hot rolls to its patron's tables. Her desire was to see new things and love life. Oh, how I miss those spontaneous adventures with my mom.

Another fond memory I have of my mother is her weekly routine of

SHE WANTED MORE

always watching her daytime stories and Golden Girls. Many of my friends laugh at me when I tell them that out of everything to watch on TV, it's usually Golden Girls that I will watch. I even have my daughters watching it now. It is a memory, a warm one that I share with my mom. On the many nights when I am missing her, I will turn on those four blue haired ladies and laugh my troubles away. For the most part, she has always been an amenable soft-hearted woman, until you upset her and provoked herGemini side to arise. It was the amenable side I often wished would evolve into more of a defender against her being the underdog in situations. I viewed her amenability as a weakness. Living out my twenties and into my thirties, I realized this could be more of a strength based on the circumstance. In hindsight, I have learned a lot from my mother, some good and some not so well. I will never doubt or question her love although I often doubted and questioned the methods. God would later help me work through those questions. There are so many times now as I struggle through parenthood that I think back with gratitude for every experience with my mother. Those experiences help challenge me to love and accept my children. They challenge me to seek to understand my children in such a way that they know I am there for them. As I move forward seeking more wisdom as I grow, I learn more about who my mother is and how to love and accept her as she is.

Moving along, ever so often my family took the opportunity to get away and see new things. We would all pack into the station wagon or my dad's truck and drive eight hours up I-55 to visit my family in Indianapolis. My grandparents and mom's brothers and sisterall livedthere, and I loved the road trip up there. More so, I was able to visit with the family I was so curious about. There was not much contact for several years between my mother and her family. I wanted to know who they were and understand why they weren't in our lives. There was some anger and frustration towards them. Glory to God, because he gave me the opportunity to work through those feelings later in life.

Sparkle Christine

When we would arrive to my grandparents' house, I would get to sleep in my mom's old bedroom. I would come down to breakfast in the morning to a spread of different meats and food. It was great. My granny would always make her special spaghetti, with smoked sausages. I can still smell it when I think about it. Such happy memories. My aunt and uncles would come by and we would laugh, and watch westerns with my granddaddy. I miss them all dearly. I would spend time going through old albums trying to get a sense of the family and mother I barely knew. I would enjoy the time spent away from our home and the realities there. My granny and granddaddy loved us, and I knew that from how they would tell us that. Every time we would see them, they would give us some money. Sometimes, my granny would take me shopping. I learned very early that I might not get to spend time with them, but if I asked for something of monetary value, it was easier to get that. It would not be until much later in my life that I was able to spend quality time with them both to bond on a deeper level. One summer, my grandparents and mother agreed to allow my little brother and I to come visit for a couple of weeks. My grandparents made the drive to Memphis to pick us up. We were so excited. I had not been away from my mother before and I was excited and ready for adventure. I had never spent time with my grandparents without my parents. I thought it would be a time of connecting, fun and most importantly, me not being stuck inside of the house. It is one of the memories I think on often. My eldest brother Christopher, up to that point had that privilege. I was happy to finally experience it too.

Christopher is seven years my senior. He was always the one I looked up to. You know, the older brother who is idolized by the younger siblings. Well, the plot thickens. Growing up, I didn't really know much about him. In my youthful eyes, I thought he was the one with all the freedom. He had the ear of our mother as the eldest and reigned over the rest of us. Oh, how I learned the truth years later from the source himself. Turns out, he had travelled a rough road before I was born and was

She Wanted More

destined for more of the same. That's his story and not mine, but for the purposes of my story, I want to share that the person I thought he was, and the man he turned out to be are totally different. My earliest memories of him are when he would babysit us while my mother was working. He kept my brothers and me while my mother worked. I remember him to be very quiet, sensitive and introverted. I loved him deeply even though I didn't understand him much. When I was eight years old, life changed for our little family forever, or at least in my mind's eye it did. Beatings were a normal occurrence in our house. My older brother Stephen was getting a beating by my stepfather. As typical, my mother did nothing to stop it. After the beating, my stepfather left the house. Christopher began to argue with my mother about why she would allow him to do it. I remember it like it happened yesterday. He said he was tired of watching it, grabbed some clothes and left. Little did I know he would never live with us again. The next morning after my parents left the house, Chris returned with donuts. He told my brothers and I that he loved us and left, never to return. I was crushed, scared and angry with him, my mother and my father. I felt abandoned. I felt anger towards my mother's weakness and hatred for a stepfather who could torment us in the name of discipline. Later, in life, I would be able to hear more of the story. It was then that I would be reconciled to my brother Christopher. I am not sure if my mother ever addressed that with my stepfather, or even if he cared about him leaving. That sort of thing was never discussed with us kids. It was as if our feelings didn't matter, and we were not allowed to be affected. Life went on like he was never there, and my mother allowed it. At least, that was my feelings from my perspective at the tender age of eight. Keep moving, keep going, feel nothing and carry on was the expectation. I learned it early in life, and as many things it has been one of the toughest struggles in my fight to unpacking my stuff.

I would always remember that moment when Chris stood up to my mother and left because of the abusive environment. He chose a

Sparkle Christine

different path. For the longest time, I was angry with him for it. I was angry that he left us. He could no longer protect us in my opinion. Many years later, he would move to Nashville where my family and I lived. We would be together in proximity for the first time in over twenty years. We would have the time for conversation, fresh perspectives and healing. That one moment in time stuck with me. It would move me to fight the abuse no matter the cost. When my stepfather would rage, I would rage back hatefully. I may lose the battle, but I would go down fighting and spewing my hate for him. I would run away from home and hide behind the church in our neighborhood. My mother would always find me. I would cry that I didn't want to go back knowing that when I did, I would be beaten for running away. I lived in constant fear of the time he would come home from work. When I was in sixth grade, I received a beating for what I don't remember. I went to school angry and sad. I had bruises, which was normal given the severity of the beatings inflicted upon my brother Stephen and me. My little brother Daniel would never share the same experience. To this day, I am not sure why. I always felt it was because Lawrence was his father, while Stephen and I were the stepchildren. However, I arrived at school that day with fresh bruises. My teacher uncovered what happened and soon Child Protective Services took me out of the home for a time. Eventually they sent me back to return to the same life. I remember receiving a call from my grandmother shortly after my return home. She was furious with me. That day, she told me that no matter what happens in my house, I was to never tell anyone about it. I was again deflated. Did no one see injustice as I did?

So much of what we undergo as children shape our self-narratives, and what we think of ourselves as we shift into adulthood. I have been blessed to have been provided an array of therapists, advisors, mentors and praying church mothers to help me sort through those narratives from my youth. Of the advice given, one of the most impactful has been to have compassion for those who aided in the traumatic situations that

SHE WANTED MORE

occurred to me. Compassion, a word I was not familiar with, was rarely used in our home growing up. I will tell you what I initially thought of that piece of advice. To many of those same advisors I just spoke of with such love, I suggested that they keep their advice, and if they wanted to keep me as a client, friend or mentee to never ask something of that magnitude of me again. Funny enough, it was their compassion for me that led them to stick through that uncomfortable moment and ultimately help me see the light. The very definition of compassion directs the reader to feel sympathy for another person's sorrow or distress. All I knew was that I was the person who needed compassion, because of the sorrow my mother allowed my stepfather to cause. In retrospect, I still had quite a road to travel before grace would abound in my heart for my stepfather, and even that of my mother. Quite a while ago, I wrote out every single feeling and emotion I could remember feeling as a child. Then, I wrote out the new feelings and emotions I felt as an adult having undergone extensive therapy, finding God's love and my place in the Kingdom, and living a bit longer to understand the compassion adults need when dealing with difficult situations. The vast contrast in the feelings felt then, versus now was a shocking realization of how those self-narratives we form early in our lives can affect our own feelings of self-worth. The list I created was confirmation for me that writing this book could give someone hope.

2

Losing My Way

SCHOOL WAS MY ESCAPE FROM HOME AND EQUALLY TRAUMATIC AT TIMES. I enjoyed the attentions of my teachers. Praise for my accomplishments and level of ability were a common occurrence. I remember wanting to work hard to make them proud. I felt a carnal need inside of me to make sure someone saw that I was worth more than a cursory glance. The schoolwork itself came easy to me. It was the social skills and interactions with my peers that would incite an anxiety attack throughout my life at the memory of school. Each semester ending would bring more "Principal List" awards and favor amongst the staff. Equally, this would bring as much pain as it did pleasure. Growing up poor was one thing. Growing up poor with it being noticeable in school was another. For as long as I could remember, getting ready for school meant preparing to be teased for how I

SHE WANTED MORE

dressed, smelled, and for the house we lived in. Today as a parent, I can look back on it and have compassion on my mother as she said all the things, I have been guilty of saying to my own kids. She would say what she deemed to be encouraging words such as, "don't worry," or "ignore them."

One of the most difficult parts of therapy has been walking myself back through those tough life situations that we somehow numb out into a place of nonexistence before we reach adulthood. I chose to numb out the incessant bullying, tears and the depressive state I sunk into as a result. Even today as I write, recalling the school years cause physical pain. I am sure you are not surprised when I say that the bullying led me into some very dark places. That young girl from all those years ago viewed herself from the perspective of others. During my school years, complexion gave some the ability to rank your importance or value you could offer. I am what some would say amongst People of Color, dark skinned. Somehow, I ranked low, and even lower because of our poor beginnings. Over the course of time, I began to buy into the image projected upon me by my peers. Today, I can proudly look at myself in the mirror and soundly say I feel beautiful and confident in my own skin.

Let's talk about this thing called Social Anxiety. When I was in school, there was not a name for what we today call social anxiety. Social anxiety is the fear of being judged and evaluated negatively by other people, leading to feelings of inadequacy, inferiority, self-consciousness, embarrassment, humiliation, and depression. When I was introduced to the concept, I felt as if a dam had been released inside of me. It was almost as if something normalized the ticking emotional time bomb in my body. I was 32 years old when I learned that I too had social anxiety. According to a 2007 ADAA (Anxiety and Depression Association of America) survey, 36% of people with social anxiety disorder report experiencing symptoms for 10 or more years before seeking help. I am sure that from the outside, my 32-year-old self-did not appear to struggle with this. I was the woman who managed sales teams, led

Sparkle Christine

meetings, and attended networking events as often as I changed suits. This was also the woman who felt small twinges of terror in the pit of her stomach each time she had to walk into a room surrounded by people, join a company conference call, introduce herself to a team of clients, and give presentations to her team. This my friends, is social anxiety. Silent tears of agony when you spend your life worrying about someone else's judgement of you. So why the concern, you ask? Quite often, social anxiety is something developed over the course of time as a result of experiences during your formative years. The trauma experienced during my younger years that involved teasing because of my complexion, or due to our menial housing situation created a space where I gravitated towards feelings of inadequacy, inferiority and self-doubt. That means, no matter what boardroom I walked into and commanded, or awards earned, the little girl who was tormented and teased would resurface when faced with social situations.

Somewhere between the summer of 7th and 8th grade, my mother made a very brief, but courageous attempt to regaining balance. She moved away from my stepfather, and with that shift brought about a new school for me and my siblings. I found myself in a new school and new environment. I was ready to reinvent myself. Keep in mind this new school was a full, say ten miles from my previous one. For the naïve girl I was, that meant much farther than I was to eventually find out. I set out to right all the wrongs and create a new Sparkle. Enters in the first mistake, take note. I would be fun, loving and popular. How many of you are shaking your head as you read this? Yes, I was sorely mistaken, but here it goes. The first day of school, the teacher asks those same questions that you hear year after year. This time, for the first time since I began school, I asked to be called by Christine. Sparkle, my given name had failed me time and time again. All I knew was, no one loved Sparkle. She had no friends, was constantly teased, didn't have any school crushes (or none that returned the feelings), and was overall an unlovable waste of life. Christine was ready to break out of her shell and

SHE WANTED MORE

do whatever she needed to do for people to like her. Enters the second mistake. Here is what I didn't count on. In the small town of Millington, TN, everyone knows each other, and in some way related. Moving from Woodstock Elementary to Millington Middle School with only a few miles difference was not going to give me enough distance to not be known. That didn't go so well, especially when I was called out by another student who also transitioned from my previous school with me. What are the odds?!

The message in that example, is that my internal insecurity caused me to have the belief that I was unlovable, useless and not worthy of real relationships. How my heart hurts for that little girl. The woman looking back can sense the internal struggles at acceptance, not only by her peers, but self-acceptance as well. How many times have you fed into the idea that to be accepted, you must conform or reinvent a generic version of yourself? I became good at that. At least, I thought I did. I would say and do all the things I thought may work to help me fit in with not only the popular kids, but any group that would accept me. This led me into further depression. I was still battling a very unstable home life and balancing it with school trauma. What was a girl to do? I will tell you what I did. I started smoking cigarettes. By that time, it was easy to get people to buy them for me. I was 13 years old and developed a smoking habit. I would carry my cigarettes with me to school each day. As soon as the bell would ring to signal the end of the day, I would hurriedly leave school and find a solitary place in the neighborhood, pull out my pack and smoke my day away. It was downhill from there. After one particularly stressful day full of tears, self-hatred, and endless teasing, I said to heck with it all. I crossed the street, turned around and looked at the assistant principal who was safely directing the mean kids whom I hated dearly across the street, pulled out my cigarettes and lit up. He, of course, was shocked. At that point, I was a straight A student on the path to becoming a drop out because I could not take it anymore. I didn't care and it was essentially

Sparkle Christine

my, "F" you moment to him, the school and those evil kids.

That day I learned that you could get suspended for smoking cigarettes off school grounds, if they saw you smoking. I am not sure how it all played out, the memory is lax on that, but I know that I disappointed a lot of people that day. I disappointed the staff that believed in me, even if they couldn't help me navigate the bullying, I was subject to. I can remember my mother not saying much about that. She knew I was being bullied, yet she could not figure out how to help me. I don't blame her as I knew she was limited in possessing the necessary tools to walk me through overcoming those hurdles. She loved me with everything she had inside of her.

The rest of that school year consisted of becoming a pro at avoiding people, hiding the fact that I was smoking cigarettes and a suicide attempt. It wasn't my first, and sadly it was not going to be my last time. There were some bright spots. I have the memory of learning to speak German. I always liked a good challenge, and learning is what I excelled at. So, instead of choosing Spanish or French like many of the kids I knew, I chose to take German. It still brings a smile to my face today. It was a fun, challenging moment in time that I remember fondly. That doesn't mean you should approach me after reading this expecting fluency. Like many other things, that moment in time passed quickly and with it any knowledge I had of the culture and language.

Pills were always something I could easily access in my home. My mother had lots of medication. She was careful not to have them lying around, but I was what you called back then full of mischief, and maybe a little bit of strife depending on who you talked to. If I wanted to do something, that little stubborn piece of me was going to do it regardless of what anyone did to stop me. Today, we call that little CEOs in training. By then, the cigarettes and alcohol I discovered were not working much anymore. I started regularly taking pills to numb out. I had gotten to the point where I didn't need a moment of depression or

She Wanted more

suicidal thinking to drug myself. It didn't matter what it was or where it came from. In 9th grade, I decided to take ROTC to avoid P.E. with some of the girls who had made my life a living hell during grade school. Can you believe it? I thought life in ROTC was easier than struggling to climb a rope while being called, "blackey" by groups of kids. Boy, was I wrong. It was tough, but it became a small bright spot in my life. I found a couple of kids who accepted me into their fold. They were all misfits of some sort just like me. Struggling to be strong while silently battling life at home and school as we all knew it to be. For the first time in my school life, I felt semi safe. We all had another thing in common. We liked pills. One of the kids' younger sister was battling cancer at St. Jude. He would steal her medication and bring them to school. We would all take them during drill practice in the afternoons. Any extras would go into our pockets for after dinner treats at home.

My mother knew something wasn't right. I never knew how she found out that I was buying energy pills from the gas station in the mornings on the way to school to get high. Call it mother's intuition, or maybe the fact that I was so high I could barely see straight. She pleaded with me to stop getting high, even took my pills when she found them on me. Those were the days I was too high to remember to hide them from her. Part of me didn't care if she found them. I wanted her to know. I wanted her to see how much pain I was in. She needed to see how life had broken me down, hurt me, shattered anything I thought was ever good about life. Pain had turned to anger, and anger turned to rage.

I didn't stop. I refused to listen. I OVERDOSED.

I remember it so clearly as if it happened yesterday. I was at school that day. I had taken a pill that morning to get me through my classes, especially Algebra, the only class I have ever failed in my life. I was so stressed that day that I could not feel the effects. Looking back, I am sure my tolerance was so high that I needed more to reach the high I wanted. I was an addict at 14, and I needed more. I took another pill.

Sparkle Christine

That did it. It really did it. I was higher than I had ever been. But this was different. I was too high. Even worse, my mother was picking me up from school soon. She knew something was wrong as soon as I got in the car. This could have been because I could not see clearly. Everything was a haze. I remember getting home and beginning to shake. I knew I was going to die. All I could hear was my mother saying, "I told you to stop. I told you to stop." What she didn't know was how far away she sounded, almost a whisper. I had never been so afraid in my life. That night I shivered and shook, vomited and convulsed. I laid in her bed in her arms begging her to take me to the hospital.

She said no. She refused to take me to the hospital. My mother said I had to feel every bit of it, so that I would not do it again. Three things happened that day, I developed a fear of overdosing, I stopped taking pills for a couple of years to pick up marijuana, and something inside of me shattered. It's been several years since that happened. I have come to understand more about my mother as a woman and person.However, the day the overdose occurred, something broke inside me and it was many years before it healed. In fact, it wasn't until my thirties that it did. When I asked my mother to take me to the hospital because I thought I would die, she refused. The girl felt unloved. In that moment, I felt that she would have allowed me to die without a care because she saw me at my lowest and in distress and did not try to save me. The woman I am now, tries to see it from her perspective of teaching me a lesson, in the typical fashion lessons were taught to kids where I came from. I vividly remember her holding me through my shakes, which now I can see as love from her. She loved me the only way she knew how to love, toughly. The mother I started out as was just as tough. With God, I was able to grow in my understanding of what I should be tough about, and what I should not be tough about, but to do it all in love and kindness. This is still a challenge, but I get up every day trying to be better than I was before.

As I reminisce, I am grateful God still had work for me to do. It was one

She Wanted More

of the moments that shaped the testimony I share with you today. During that space in my life, I was not sure why my body wouldn't die, because everything else was numb. I began to question why God had allowed so many things to happen to me. I felt dirty, ashamed and worthless. I ran away from home that summer and joined a gang. I lived with a friend and her family, moved my boyfriend in and started smoking and drinking to forget about the dreams I once had to attend an HBCU (Historically Black College and University) and become a lawyer. My mother would come over to bring me clothes and food whenever she could. She had to hide that from my stepfather, who called the police when I left. I swore her to secrecy on my whereabouts for both my safety and hers at least that is how I felt. I grew up a lot that summer and in so many ways. For one, I had my innocence taken away. It was two years prior that I had be introduced to sex. Oh no, I was to lose the innocence of childhood. It was that summer I learned the real meaning of hunger. I was too young to work, so I had to learn other ways to take care of myself. I learned to hustle, I learned to lie, and I learned to think about me and only me. My boyfriend was 19, and let's just say I was much younger, and we met as members of the same local gang. This was the summer my life changed from getting a beating from my stepfather to getting hit by my boyfriend. He knew he had control from the first slap. Why would I leave? Being hit or hurt had been my life's narrative. Nothing had changed, except now, I had the choice to decide who to accept it from. Besides, I wasn't going home because I was too afraid of what my stepfather would do because I left in the first place.

That domestic abuse from my boyfriend continued for a few more months. One day, my mother came to see me and begged me to come home. I was worn out, sad, depressed, addicted to marijuana and alcohol, abused, yet I refused to go back home. Anything was better than life at home. At least there, I had a choice. At home, there was no choice. Because she loved me, she found an apartment for my boyfriend

Sparkle Christine

and me to live in a better part of town. I was underage, so she put it in her name and off we went to live a little closer to her. We didn't have jobs and couldn't keep up with the bills. I will always remember the day I gave up and went home. My boyfriend would leave for days at a time. This day I was all alone, and surely drunk. He finally came back. I was watching the news and trying to ignore the fact that he had been gone for days. It was September 11, 2001. Something about seeing the attacks on the country and watching the planes made me go into a panic. I needed my mother. In that moment, I was a scared teenager who had taken on life too soon and I just wanted the safety of my mother's arms. Besides, I needed to get away from this guy I had roped myself onto.

I finally went home. The straps tightened from my stepfather as expected, but I was just glad to be able to sleep without fear of wondering where I would get my next meal. At least they fed me was my thought. That only lasted a few months. I told my mother I wasn't going back to school. By then, I think she was afraid I'd leave again if she pushed too hard. She conceded and enrolled me in homeschool. I received my high school diploma through homeschool, before I found out I was pregnant. I would have my daughter later that year. Before I could share my pregnancy, and it was my plan to only say something when I started to show, I was hit with some hard news. A familiar conversation reared its ugly head. We were getting evicted, again. Once again, my parents weren't the best money managers. They taught us to work hard, but to manage nothing. They did the best they could with what they knew, but never learned how to manage themselves financially. With nowhere to go, my parents found a trailer park that had weekly rentals. It was there that I shared my pregnancy. My mother cried but said nothing, my stepfather cried and told me I could get my belly button pierced if I aborted my baby. I refused. I finally could have something love me back. I was keeping my baby. I don't think he ever loved me the same again. The funny thing is, I know and still know to

She Wanted more

this day he loved me. He loved me in the way he thought I should be loved, just like he was. He came from an era of beatings and tough decisions, respect and obedience. He commanded that from my mother right on down to us kids. Was that the best decision in raising kids? No, but today I choose to walk in forgiveness and healing.

So, the trailer park was only temporary. Yet again, my parents were unable to quiet their own demons to consistently pay the rent. We moved on to a hotel. My stepfather moved in with his family. So, there it began. My mother, my two brothers and my pregnant self were living in the Admiral Bimbo Motel on Summer Avenue in Memphis. That place has since been demolished, and along with it the memories of more innocence lost. Because of our lifestyle, I was sick most of the time and could not work. My older and younger brother saw my mother struggling and began to do what they could to help. That is their story to tell, but I will say that innocence was lost. I don't know if they know it, but I have so much respect for the men they have become today, because they too had to sacrifice growing up just to live.

I felt like I had to do my part too. When I decided to write this book, I had to make some tough decisions. One of those decisions was to be as open as I could to paint the picture of where I have been in my life. I wanted to show you where I was and where I am going. That means a nakedness I have never felt, until now. I was pregnant, watching my mother do her best to pay the weekly hotel rental. My brothers stopped going to school from what I can remember. I felt even more worthless than I had in all my life. She and my brothers fed us, paid the room fees and kept us safe. I don't think I have to tell you about the dangers of living on the streets. Even pregnant, I seemed to have caught the eye of one of the dealers who also stayed at the hotel. Apparently, it was easier to deal from a hotel room than a house or apartment. I felt a responsibility to help my family. I started dating the guy. He had money, we needed help. If any of you knew me personally, you would understand the pain felt in me having to say that or even do it. I was

Sparkle Christine

young, stressed, pregnant and scared. Please be kind to me in your judgement. He took care of my family and me for a time. Luckily, my mother, in her awesomeness, was able to find us a place to live within a week of me going into labor nearly two months earlier than my daughter's original due date. With the move came the beginning of a small ray of light that I felt God gave me in my heart. There may be a way out. I might be able to succeed. Life can start anew. I wanted life to be different, especially with me becoming a mother.

3

Adulting Times Two

PICTURE IT. CRYING BABY. CRYING TEEN MOTHER. A FULL HEART. No one told me an infant could eat so much, never sleep and cry for no apparent reason. Even with that, the love I felt she had for me was deeper than anything that has ever pulled on my heart strings. I was confused on how to parent this little creature, but I loved her more than words could ever describe. She was my person. She would love me in a world that hadn't loved me at all. I would protect her, because that is what I thought love was. Love was security. At any rate, all I had was my opinion, and in a world of opinions, only mine mattered. I learned this firsthand when my grandmother visited my baby for the first time with my great aunt in tow. She looked at my daughter, and God rest her soul, said something that would hurt for many years. She looked back at my aunt and said, "You will be just like your mother and have more babies." I cannot communicate the physical pain felt from such a statement. I vowed then that I would prove her and the world wrong. I

Sparkle Christine

would succeed. I created my family. That is all that mattered. What could go wrong now? As fate would have it, plenty could go wrong, and it did. When my daughter was two months old, a few days after her father visited with her for the first time, the phone rang. It was his mother calling in the middle of the night. He had been shot and was in the intensive care unit at the local hospital. I hurriedly woke my mother and she took me to the hospital. There I sat by his side, helping to suction his spit valves and other things to keep me busy and not thinking for the two days I was there until I was asked to leave by his mother. Over the next few days, any hopes of him leaving there to continue healing at home left me. He died. He was 21 years old. There I sat a young mother devastated that her daughter would have to grow up wondering who her father was. Even more so, it hurt knowing I would one day have to explain to her how he died. Somehow, the trauma from that gave me a fear of dying young. I was afraid I would not live passed 21. In retrospect, I was able to see this as a defining moment to add to the hopelessness I felt in my life. Thankfully, my mother was right there to help me through that challenging time. She was instrumental in picking up the pieces, while keeping my daughter close to her in the process.

As time went on, I adjusted to motherhood while also trying to navigate where to go from where I was. My mother continued to babysit my daughter as I joined the workforce and enrolled in a nearby business college. I would catch the bus to school and work in the work study program after classes. The evening classes I attended helped with being able to work during the day at different waitressing jobs. I wasn't afforded much time with my daughter due to the schedule I maintained to take care of us. I saw it as sacrifice and consequence. It was my sacrifice to provide for the love of my life, and consequence for the difficult route I chose to take in life. My daughter spent much of her time with her grandmother. Without her care, I would not be where I am today. A teen pregnancy can go one of two ways, and support is key.

SHE WANTED MORE

The instructors at the school continued to breathe life into me when I wanted to quit. In fact, I did quit one semester soon before I was to finish. The Dean over the department brought my dry bones back to life with her encouragement. Something shifted in me during the last six months of my time there. I began to dream. Typically, I did not allow myself to think past what is, to what could be. That could be disappointment just waiting to happen. Where I come from there are no dreams, only harsh cold reality. It was the first time I allowed myself to think past my current reality to a slim possibility of a different life. Up to the time of graduation, I had drifted through waitressing jobs and floated from place to place. I was curious as to what this little piece of hope was. I wanted to discover more. Could it be? Could I do something to make my daughter proud? If I knew one thing it was this, if I wanted it, I was going to get it at all cost. So, what did I want? I wanted to be free; I just wasn't sure what I wanted to be free from.There was God again, pricking me in the quiet places. So, I did what was customary to me when that happened. I turned the noise up louder, because I wasn't ready to hear the call.

I landed my first office gig in the business office of a car dealership. I was out of school and able to spend more time with my daughter. I am sure my mother was grateful for that. She had taken on therole of mother to her while I went out in the world trying to find myself. I like to think of myself as a "check the boxes" type of person. I needed some formal educational training to support my family, check. Employment, check. Trusted babysitter while I go out and make it all happen, check. That's it, right? What else is needed? I soon found out. Buried not so deep under the surface was the pain of the past, and a bit of the present. The same social anxiety and depression I suffered as a child was still looming in my face daily. Not to mention, the drug use from adolescence followed me. The only difference now was I becameaddicted to substances other than pills. I had a PH. D. in numbing out. I began to mentally decline. Like most of us parents, we

Sparkle Christine

take care of the children, the home and the checklist. Where are we, where was I? I was on the heels of a massive depressive break. Long story short, I had a breakdown and willingly checked myself in a mental health facility. With my previous suicide attempts, I knew this would get worse before it got better if I didn't get help. Where was God I wondered? Looking back, I know he was right there. A friend materialized out of nowhere and stood by my side through the entire process. My super woman mother was still there to take care of my daughter, even as her own demons chased her. I got the care I needed, went home and worked to rebuild my mind. Keep in mind I was still running from the one who would make it clear.

Not only was I running in mind, I started physically running. My first stop was Phoenix, AZ. I was dating one of my brother's friends. After a year or so we decided to move away from Memphis. We packed up my daughter, all our belongings and began a 2-day journey to Arizona. That didn't last long. It was too hot and too far away from anything familiar in my life. My daughter and I were both ready to return after a few short months. Back in Memphis, I headed to work, and assumed life as I knew it. Schooling, check. Job, check. Healthy relationship, epic fail. If there was any kryptonite I had, it was men. I have always been in love with the thought of being in love. I learned to have a critical eye at the world, but not so much when it comes to men. That was my soft spot. Somewhere deep down under the regret, rejection and fear was a little girl wanting desperately to be loved and protected. Oddly enough, I thought I would find that love in a man instead of God. As things go, I tried to do just that. I desperately moved from bad relationship to worse, looking for someone to save me from myself. After a few attempts, I met who would become my first husband. As I sit here and write, I have now gone through my second divorce. My first husband's name was Guyana. He was a smooth talking, energetic jokester with tattoos covering his body. I met him in the local tobacco store. We were inseparable from the moment we met. He was the Yin to my Yang, and I

She Wanted More

was in love at first sight, young love. Many have said the same of him. Our love was so complicated that we would often fight in the same great passion that we would love. I smile to think of the day's past. After such an electrifying connection, I moved him in within weeks. The false sense of security I had been so great at giving myself when I was in a relationship with a man returned.

Two months later, I announced to Guy that I was moving to Minnesota where my birth father, my brother Stephen and my father's other children were. Memphis was draining me. There were not enough opportunities, but plenty of bad choices. I wanted better for me and my child. In typical Sparkle fashion, I gave him the option of staying or going. Even worse, I was leaving within three days of announcing my decision. He decided to leave with us. I left my mom the house and everything in it, hopped a Greyhound bus with two bags for my child and me, and headed to start my new life. I arrived in Minnesota in December that year. No one could have prepared me for what greeted me that day. It was cold and immediately I started to regret my decision. My big brother met us at the bus station and whisked us off to his home as we started our new life. He blessed my life that day. It was tough, but the opportunity to start over and create a new life for my daughter and myself was a defining moment I will never forget. I spent four years in Minneapolis. During that time period, I was able to reconcile things with my father. I learned more about the man who remained a mystery throughout my youth. I learned things I wanted to know, and a lot I didn't. I met some of my siblings for the first time in my life. I am grateful for every experience and insight gained from that time period. It taught be a lot about who I was as a person, and how generational curses or repeated behaviors can be passed through bloodlines. Being able to spend that time, although very short, with my father was a necessary component in my healing later in life. My father would die in 2012 from cancer, a year after I returned to Memphis. Guy and I got married two years into the move. In 2011, we separated, and

Sparkle Christine

he transitioned back to Tennessee. I would follow him shortly thereafter, in hopes of working through our marital issues. Even then, there was part of me that desperately wanted God to bless our union. At that time, divorce was not an option. I gave up my new life and returned home to Tennessee to fix my marriage. Ultimately, we divorced, and a couple years later he died.

When I moved to Minnesota, it was the first time I had been able to fully parent my daughter. From her birth, I had to go to work to support her. When I wasn't working, I would do everything I could to still enjoy pieces of my life when I could. She was left with my mother most of the time. It was a blessing and curse. Over the course of time, she slipped away from being my daughter to more of my mothers and brothers' child. We would live together, but when she was apart from them, she cried. Her bond became stronger with my mother and not me. I longed for my child to have that with me. I was jealous. It surfaced in how I interacted with both my mother and daughter. I could not discipline her or instruct her in much when my mother was around. Looking back, I can clearly see how my mother wanted to help her child raise a child. She had the wisdom and patience I lacked, and she stepped in to help. I was impatient, downright belligerent at times, and unwilling to see her viewpoint. My daughter was four years old when we moved to Minnesota. I refer to that time as the beginning of our relationship. It was then that I started to grow up and accept full responsibility of her, not just financial responsibility.

All the while, I was still struggling to develop my parenting skills. Becoming a teen parent did not help my stages of growth into adulthood. One of the things that greatly suffered was my emotional intelligence when dealing with children at different life stages. My oldest daughter received the short end of the stick with my parenting. When I started experiencing her terrible twos, and help me God, threes, I knew one way. The way I grew up being treated. I am not proud of the person I was during that time. I parented with a heavy hand of force and

She Wanted More

aggression. Redemption and grace are the foundation I stand on today. How grateful I am for grace. Looking back, I made many mistakes with both of my girls. I didn't realize how easy it was to gravitate towards what you were taught as a child. I was learning as I went. Even then God had a hand in it. He placed me around those whose presence could help me navigate things I was not instructed in as a child. Today, I still struggle with the appropriate responses and how I should parent my girls. Thank God for the many wise people he placed in my life to provide guidance.

My family were not big communicators. It usually played out like this. They told us what to do, and we did it. If we did not do it, swift punishment followed. It was that knock-you-to-the-ground or where did that hand come from so quickly kind of swift. My childhood was one where the children were to be seen and not heard. If you're reading this and you are a parent, you know we don't live in the same world today. Love, grace and patience are my daily prayers to rebuke the force, aggression and anger of the generational curses that haunt me at times. Leave it to your youngest child to test those prayers. When she came along, life and maturity had settled upon me. My eldest would challenge me and say there is too much grace and patience now. There were many times I walked in shame with how little I knew as a parent then versus today. We would have exchanges on it, and it would bring me to my knees. I'd have to call my mother and apologize for making her life much harder with my stubborn and disrespectful attitude at times. Friends, I want to encourage you today. Give yourself grace over the person you were yesterday versus today. That person did the best with the knowledge, insight and training they had. Growth is a process. Your yesterday was not ready for today, and today you aren't ready for tomorrow. Trust the process. I am a living testimony that it works. Matthew 6:34 says, "Therefore don't worry about tomorrow, because tomorrow will worry about itself. Each day has enough trouble of its own."

Sparkle Christine

Marriage has always been a goal in my life. I saw my mother and stepfather remain unhappily married since I was young. I used to say, my mother taught us how to be married, and to stay that way. Unfortunately, being happy was not part of that lesson. With that always in the back of my mind, I would never meet guys and enjoy casual dating. Where I came from, there was no casual dating. You met, you fell in love (or lust) and you got married. Simple. End of story. I went into a deep depression after the downfall of my first marriage. Amid the depression, I met my soon to be my second child's father, and second husband. Enters in another smooth-talking confident man. Are you seeing the pattern here? Well I didn't for many years. That arrogant, confident man I had a knack for being attracted to never seem to work in my favor. His name was Eddie. My brother worked for him in his restaurant and introduced us. He came into my life when I was low, recovering from heartache, and not entirely sure if I was going to keep healing or return to my then husband. Enters in Eddie with roses. I've always been a woman after a rose. He gifted me with white roses on Valentine's Day, and our romance began. In the beginning, we would talk business, stocks, bonds and current events. He stirred my mind and my body. This was different than before. I felt awakened in my mind, but it also awakened my body. Nine years after the birth of my eldest daughter, I became pregnant. Our daughter, Madison was born and three years later we were married. In between those years, there would be multiple separations. There was a time when I moved back in with my parents. My daughters and I would live with them for a year as I worked my way out of another setback. The second marriage was tougher than the first. My husband was ex-military, from Orange Mound in Memphis, and much like the first man I married. The only difference this time was the level of physical abuse the children and I suffered. We loved hard and fought even harder. Years later, I would work through understanding how I would attract similar personalities. What a shock when I learned, that was the result of fallacy within me, not them. Can anyone relate? Can you guess what happened to us?

SHE WANTED MORE

That's right, we divorced.

I now had two children, nine years apart. Both needed care, love and guidance. That meant, gone were the days when I packed a few bags and left my life behind. I promised them I would stabilize our lives and provide whatever the cost. A few months before I gave birth, I found employment with a hotel company. I worked in the file room. One day, the VP of Sales & Marketing approached me about a position as her Executive Assistant. Of course, I wanted out of the file room, so I accepted the job. I was grateful and surprised at the offer. That VP will always carry a special place in my heart. Through her, God began a special work in me. In that moment, he began preparing me for such a time as this. I digress. I wouldbegin working for her, leave to have my daughter, and return six weeks later to my position. Over the course of time, I became an expert at learning hotel sales from the corporate level. Eventually, the company would prepare to relocate offices to Atlanta, GA. I would remain in Memphis and begin working with a large hotel as the Administrative Assistant to five salespeople, all women. It was there that I would fall in love with on-property sales. I also learned I was pretty good at it too. What I didn't know was that God was changing me from the inside out, one sales call at a time. Up to that point, because of my social anxiety, I would not openly talk to people I did not know. I was extremely uncomfortable if I had to speak with the attention of others upon me. Sales training was just the thing to push me outside of myself. I often joke, once you have been trained into hotel sales, there is nothing that could embarrass you after that. The industry was key in the process of developing my skills for God.

I finally got the breakthrough I had been waiting for. God granted me favor, and I was promoted into management. In the past, it was a struggle trying to figure out what I could do to bring sustainable income to my family. Through it all, I had developed one specific prayer. I prayed that God would give me the means to support my children. I not only asked that he allow and provide a way for me to support them, but

Sparkle Christine

to support them without the aid of someone else's resources. By that, I meant a man's assistance. No, that does not mean I was bitter. I wanted him to show me I could do it through him, and not have to depend on man. I don't know about you, but my ability to support myself has swung the scales in different directions when dealing with men in the past. I no longer wanted to operate in that mindset. It was time to grab those big girl panties and stand alone. I remember the day I felt that prayer answered. I was overcome with surprise, joy and gratitude. There weren't many answered prayers in my life, so that one took me by surprise. God was not only answering prayers, he was building my faith. He was creating a path, and he would light the way. There was not only a promotion, but mentorship. It is my belief that there is power in the blessings not prayed or asked for. I knew the need to provide a life for my children. There I sat, no bachelor's degree, but with the favor of the Lord I received a position only graduates received at the time. At the time, I did not know I would need certain tools instilled in me along the way. After many years of placing myself at the "adult" table to eat, I was finally ready to digest the meal. The wheels in my life werebeginning to turn into purpose. I knew that was what I needed to push me to the next level in my life. I wasn't prepared for the level of awakening it would bring. I was beginning to evolve into a different person, far different from anything I thought I would or could be.

4

Learning the Strongholds

2 Corinthians 10: 3-6

"For though we live in the world, we do not wage war as the world does. The weapons we fight with are not the weapons of the world. On the contrary, they have divine power to demolish strongholds. We demolish arguments and every pretension that sets itself up against the knowledge of God, and we take captive every thought to make it obedient to Christ. And we will be ready to punish every act of disobedience once your obedience is complete."

MY LIFE ALWAYS FELT LIKE ONE BIG HOLDING PATTERN. I would dig my way out of one situation, and months later find myself

Sparkle Christine

smack in the middle of another one similar. What am I cursed? That is what I would always ask myself. Nearly four years ago, I took some time to reflect on my life and figured out that I was in fact cursed. No, this is not the point in the story where you stop reading. In fact, I challenge you to open yourself up to a different way of thinking. Just walk with me here for a few moments. I think you will find it more relatable than you would have originally thought. The scriptures reference strongholds over fifty times in the Bible. Why then do we not understand its place in our lives? I was tired of being tired and I set out on a mission to figure out why I always ended up in the same scenario in different seasons. It was great being able to read in the Bible about demolishing strongholds. But for the person I was then who read the scriptures with limited understanding, I needed to know specifically what strongholds were and how acquiring that knowledge could help me overcome them. Pondering that sentiment alone provoked me to reflect on what the Word meant in my life. Let's see. A stronghold is something you can't shake. It is something that keeps rearing its ugly head no matter what you do to keep it at bay. When it surfaces, it might look differently than the last time it came up, but the root is the same. The more I broke it down, the more my interest was peaked on uncovering what it was. Throughout my life, I had experienced more than my share of heartache and strife. Could it be I had some curses over me and in my spirit that I needed to break? How could I break them, if I wasn't clear on what they were? In that small whisper, God said it was time to figure it out.

The first thing I needed to do was understand where I was in life. What did I feel? On the surface, I felt hindered by fear, shame, regret and uncertainty. I was in pain from rejection, not feeling safe and the lack of will to move forward in my life. I was in the middle of my holding pattern trying to dig myself out. Each setback brought me closer and closer to the brink of depletion. Each hurt and shameful memory caused me to frequently repeat the cycle of familiar circumstances. Somehow, I thought I would achieve a different result, with the same strategy. If

She Wanted more

that was the surface, what lay beneath it? What did I need to do to find the root and dig it out? My life depended on it. I began to feel a deep-seeded longing for freedom. I knew in my heart there was more for me somewhere, I just didn't know where to look. I had spent my life wrestling and fighting for a chance at life. Why did I feel like I was fighting with life and myself? I would look up to see the self-sabotage of the very thing I fought for, or against, and wonder what it was all about.I didn't know, but I knew I had to find out. As God would have it, he was just about to show me. He used my aunt to show me the door. It was up to me to open it and search for what I would learn to be my strongholds.

My aunt Linda and I did not have a close relationship while I was growing up. Today, she is my best friend. There had always been some unspoken tension between my mother and her, so our relationship was nonexistent until I was in my thirties. I am happy to say all is resolved with them and I love them dearly for it. I like to think our union was another power play by God. My grandfather was ill, and we began to communicate during that time. God graciously restored, repaired and made anew our relationship. She became a bright spot in my life, and an example of a godly woman after his own heart. In my own way, I idolized her. Here was a woman with a testimony of her own, proudly walking in the calling God had on her life. She knew my fresh, new desire to follow Christ. She began to push and challenge me to not just talk about it, but to be about it. Aside from the people who studied the Bible with me, no one else challenged me to examine every imperfect piece of myself for God's glory. I was at the point in my second marriage where all hell was breaking loose. I would call my aunt crying about the latest thing he had done expecting sympathy and comfort. I would get them, but with an extra dose of look in the mirror, Sparkle. How had I gotten to this point? I told her about a book I had gotten from my oldest daughter's aunt. It was a John Eckhardt book on strongholds and curses. My aunt decided then and there as she prayed in the Spirit that this was

Sparkle Christine

something I needed to dive further into.

At my core what were the things that came up repeatedly like a broken record? Anger, anxiety, depression, addiction, codependency and sex. You can't see me shuddering as I write this but trust me, I am doing it. I have a confession to make. This was the last chapter I decided to write in the book. I did this because it is the hardest one for me to share with you. I am opening myself up completely and allowing you to see the core weaknesses in my life. It is no easy thing to do. Even more so, they are the things that have been the toughest for me to overcome. John 8:32 says, "And you will know the truth, and the truth will set you free." I wanted to be set free. Free from making the same bad decisions. Free from feeling like I had the worth of an old disposed piece of clothing. I let those thoughts roll over me like a tidal wave. Wait a minute? I loved God. So what? I was taking care of my children. So what? I was living life the best way I knew how. And my point? The point is, no matter what fresh hell I conquered, if I did not address the root of the problems, they would always return in the form of something else. Alright, I can do this. I had to pump myself up first after identifying the core areas I needed to focus on. It now was about understanding and walking back through history to face the demons and purge my system.

Even as a young child I would experience outbursts of anger. I'm not talking about the occasional flare up from a disagreement. I am talking about blind rage. There were times where I would scare myself and not have anyone to talk to about it. I was notorious for making my brothers and stepsister miserable. I would wake up angry and go to bed angry some days. The strange part about it is I wouldn't always know why. I felt like something was wrong with me, but I just chalked it up to me being so unhappy with the things I faced at home and school. Truthfully, that played a part, but not the full part. Generational curses are also found in the Bible. In Exodus 34:7, God is being referenced as bringing forth consequences of the fathers' wrongdoing on the children and grandchildren. Many have and will continue to dispute this viewpoint.

She Wanted more

For me, I had to look at the circumstances surrounding those who came before me. My birth father was prone to force reckoning bouts of anger throughout his life. While in my mother's womb, I was exposed to them. It is often said that the baby experiences and feels what the mother does pre-birth. I can say with certainty this was a stronghold exchanged pre-birth. When my daughter was a toddler, I would find myself losing my temper over the smallest of things. As I got older, it would become increasingly worse. I did not fully confront that spirit until I was entangled in my second divorce. I would lose my cool, and immediately after, became overcome with feelings of guilt and self-hatred. When I learned it was a stronghold; I was not sure if I was to be relieved or afraid. Can you relate? Have you ever felt feelings of anger and you're not sure why? I encourage meditation and therapy to help you reflect below the surface to discovery.

My earliest memories involve feelings of depression and anxiety. I would carry around this hot ball of tension inside of my stomach. If it wasn't felt in my stomach, it would rotate to my head. Early on I began experiencing headaches. I wasn't quite sure why I had such an onslaught of pain at any given time. If I can give my mother credit for anything, let me tell you this woman kept us in the doctor's office. If we had a cough, sneeze, headache or throat pain she would whisk us off to be fixed. They could never figure my head pain out. It wasn't until years later when a specialist told me it was stress related did, I understand. In the same conversation, the anxiety and depression were addressed. I have a dear friend in my life. She is great about telling me to not call it my anxiety or my depression. If you have been able to identify any strongholds since beginning this chapter, do you find yourself calling it yours? Awareness brings about change. I noticed through the help of that friend that while praying it off my life, I was inadvertently claiming it for my life. Praying it off and sucking it back in. Revelation! We cannot speak blessings and curses from the same mouth! (James 3:10). Oh, how I was grieving the spirit! Gratitude was upon me and I began to see

Sparkle Christine

through the timeline in my family how this was another generational bind that I could and would pray and fight out of my life. For nearly twenty years I had taken different medications to ward off the symptoms of depression and anxiety. I had visited many therapists, ministers and evangelists to help combat the feelings of hopelessness. Nothing seemed to stop the cycle of that holding pattern from coming back. I would begin reliving some of the worst moments that brought me to my knees and ultimately back into the sunken places of a setback.

I learned early on how to self-medicate. Life was throwing punches I didn't quite know how to dodge yet. I needed to numb out. It went from pills to you name it. As an adult, I would clean up after a bad bout of depression and walk the path to sobriety for a few months or even years. Then something would happen. I would have marital troubles. My job would begin to experience a downturn or something in me decided I did not want to live any longer. I would be overwhelmed with being a single mother. I would somehow find my way back down the path of addiction. The interesting part about it is I may not have used the same thing to numb out. Over the course of my life, I am sad to say I have been extremely judgmental on some members of my family for their bouts of addiction. It was during those times I was the biggest fraud. I learned during the time I spent in AA that addiction is addiction, it does not matter how it appears. During the time I spent in Minnesota with my birth father before he died, he shared some sentiments on it. He said you had your addicts or junkies and you had your maintainers. The maintainers were like me. I would go to work, take care of my family, and maintain my lifestyle. When I was working or caring for the kids, I would dabble in whatever I was using to numb out at the time. I never took from the household to do it, and I made sure my family had more than enough. I wasn't an addict; I was a maintainer. I was better than those people who chose addiction over their families, or was I? I was not. I was just great at fooling myself, not even the people closest to me.

SHE WANTED MORE

Even after I came to the realization that this must be a stronghold and I must fight it as such, I did not see the real problem that needed practicals and prayer. In the hospitality industry, drinking is an unspoken norm. It is nothing for you to hit the happy hour circuit with your coworkers two to three nights a week after a long day at the office, closing deals, and working on new ones. By the time you realize your drinking has increased, you are working on one to two more bottles a night during, before, and after dinner. That was all the permission I needed to keep numbing out. The difference this time was that I was doing it because that is what we did in the industry. We had to drink to be in sales. We had to drink to maintain our million-dollar revenue goals. How could we keep our cool and our industry friendships without it? One year, I was one accident away from a D.U.I and that is when God gave me the biggest wake up call of my adult life. I had a friend who I drank with regularly. We would plan our weeks around when and how we would hook up so we could drink. We made brunch dates on the weekends, and dinner dates to drink. We even stashed away some lunch dates here and there. Even the most untrained eye would sense a problem brewing. My daughters would tag along sometimes to brunch or dinner and take note of how much drinking was involved. I was full of excuses about it being a long day, or my tolerance was high, so I needed more. I cringe to think of the example I was setting for them.

One night, I loaded up the liquor and headed over to my friend's house to have a few drinks and hang out. It was harmless in my eyes and we would just hang out for a few hours. I left the girls at home since I wouldn't be far away. Tiana was well over the age to be considered safe to babysit and be home alone. The party started. I don't remember what we were drinking that night. I know it was a good two hours and we were both completely drunk. I remember eating a little, but I was there for the drinks, so who had their mind on food? Eventually, I wanted to go home. I knew I could not drive, and my friend really shouldn't have either. Of the two of us, she was the OG of drinking. We

Sparkle Christine

decided I could come back for my car the next day. I was blackout drunk and she told me the next day she didn't remember how she got home. It had to be God, and to this day I believe that. I am grateful he spared us both and anyone driving around us. She dropped me off and the next day I was sicker than I had been when I overdosed on the pills as a teen. My daughter spent her Saturday trying to keep my youngest from coming in my room to see the mess that I was. I woke up to vomit all over my walls and bedroom. I had alcohol poisoning. I refused to go to the hospital. Sadly, the only thing I could think of was embarrassing my employer and possibly losing my job. Who knows how long they would have kept me? So, I stayed home and suffered for two days in that state. When I think back to the fear and painl inflicted on my eldest child, I am overcome with shame. God spared me and I didn't take that for granted. I had to stop abusing his grace. It was time to confront the stronghold. When I was well, I started AA meetings. Even today, I still must be cautious to avoid the same snares and traps I befell in the past with addiction. It would become a lifelong process.

While leaning in to discover the strongholds, there was one that had affected every area in my life with poison. It was codependency. Codependency is excessive emotional or psychological reliance on a partner, typically one who requires support on account of an illness or addiction. When I learned the definition, I was ready to drop the mic and exit stage left. This about summed up my entire adult life. What was that about? Okay where are the cameras? What are you trying to do to me God? I was feeling so exposed. I am one hundred percent a codependent person. To say it brought relief and trepidation. There was a word for the things I felt, but what a word it was. Immediately, my failed marriages and friendships started playing a slideshow in my brain. As a child, I would watch my mother become very bitter at my stepfather because of his drinking. She would, however, take care of him in his drunkenness as only a wife would. I never thought of how that would shape some of my behaviors into adulthood. I can see the

She Wanted More

transfer of energy from one generation to the next. I am not proud to say it, but I have encountered some of the same things with my own daughter as I watched her gravitate towards those, she feels she can help change behaviors. She learned them from me.

I recently had a conversation with my mother about the men I gravitated towards in my life. I was sharing how I have accomplished things that have given me a new set of eyes for life. However, the fresh vision was not placed on the men I naturally wanted to date. The new Sparkle cannot be with the type of men the old Sparkle wanted. These men either openly or secretly unknown to me struggled with an addiction or deep-rooted mental illness of some sort. Why would I want that type of strife in my life? I saw potential. I saw a person who was amazing once they conquered all the things that held them captive. I was in love with the thought of being in love, and by heaven or hell I would make them love me. Today, I am a single woman. That strategy didn't work too well, now did it? My mother had a clear point of view on it. She firmly said to me, "Sparkle, that is the devil and you must flee from it." She was right. It is a spirit of confusion that cannot go where God is taking me. A stronghold and a spirit that must be prayed from my life and that of my children. I found myself codependent on relationships of all kinds, not just with men. I had ungodly friendships that were based on things other than God. I would clearly hear God tell me to remove myself and I would not. I made every excuse to myself, the other people in my life who saw it, and God as to why I needed to remain in friendship with those individuals. Delayed obedience cost me. The thing about God is, if it is his will and he wants something to happen it will happen. We have two options. We can both accept it and walk in his will, or we will be brought into his will kicking and screaming. His word never comes back void. Isaiah 55:11 says, "So my word that comes from my mouth will not return to me empty, but it will accomplish what I please and will prosper in what I send it to do." He is not playing games with us and he didn't play them with me. God ended each friendship,

Sparkle Christine

and in such a way that I knew it was his doing.

The hardest stronghold to work through was sex. Initially, I didn't think it was that big of a deal. WRONG, it was the biggest deal especially if I were to be a woman after God's own heart. Hear me loud and clear. I am not here to judge anyone's circumstance, situation or choice. For me and my household, I choose a different standard and way of life. Have I always been the most upright in holding true to that? No, I have not. I am but a person and I fall short. But it is by grace I can say today I am doing all that I can in the spirit to walk the path I chose to take. I can say I was introduced to sex far earlier than most. As a result, I have had many struggles with my sexuality as an adult. I became a teen mother. I may not have had another child for nearly ten years, but the gravitation toward sex did not stop there. I was so afraid that this would carry on to my child that I actively prayed over her life to break the curse of teen pregnancy. I was the third generation of it, and I was committed to praying that spirit out of her life. Quite often where I came from, there was the confusion that to be in love meant you had to have sex.

If I didn't have sex, they wouldn't love me. Lies from the pit of hell, my friends. I was of the belief that I had to create a soul tie and give up a part of myself to be and feel loved. How many years I wasted not seeing God's love for me that I was led to believe that! 1 Corinthians 3:16-17 says, "Don't you know that you yourselves are God's temple and that God's Spirit dwells in your midst? If anyone destroys God's temple, God will destroy that person; for God's temple is sacred and you together are that temple." I had to take a couple deep breaths after that discovery. My body is God's temple, and I was freely giving it away to feel love. God had something so much greater for me. Furthermore, I could clearly see the shift in my patterns when I began to walk in God's mission for my body and not my own. Shifting, God says. I was beginning to shift. Gone were the soul ties created with every physical connection. Through grace he showed me that the physical bonds of such a stronghold were crucifying my soul. How many of you are left

SHE WANTED MORE

feeling empty after yet another decision to give more of yourself than you should in the pursuit of fulfilment?

Working through gaining the knowledge of my strongholds was no walk in the park. It was the most soul baring exercise I have ever had to do. Even more so, the work was just beginning. Figuring out the pattern is the first step. Check. Determining the root or stronghold is the next step. Check. Throughout the process, I had to learn where I stood currently in the moment of discovery. Amen for clarity. Continue to pray for it as you seek out what your strongholds are. Trust and follow the process. Give yourself some time, grace and plenty of prayer with God. Pray specifically for clarity on who you are and what your struggles are. Finally, you will be ready to work through where you want to go and what you want to be. It is ok that you may not be in that place yet, or even ready to understand what it is. Take that before God and your advisors as well. This may also be a time to seek therapy to clinically heal if needed.

When you are in a place of clarity and awareness the path to releasing the stronghold is within reach. My friends, I share my journey to offer myself up as a champion in your fight to understanding your patterns and releasing the strongholds in your life. I was able to process the shame and turn it into victory by following these steps and creating a plan of action. It ends and begins with a strong prayer life and direct relationship with our Lord and Savior. If you have made Jesus Lord over your life, you will find this process successful. You will no longer just see the way out; you will have a clear path on how to get there.

5

The Girl in the Mirror

I WAS INTO MY THIRTIES BEFORE I REALIZED I WAS IN THE MIDDLE OF AN EVOLVING IDENTITY CRISIS. There I sat, a growing professional by day, complete mess of a woman by night, crying out to God for guidance. I was in the middle of my second divorce and I could not shake the feelings of discontentment in every area of my life. For the first time, I recognized the need to understand exactly who I was. Oh yeah, I am talking about the good, bad and the downright ugly. I don't mean the surface junk, but every little disgusting crevice like those cramped little spaces between your car seat and the console. Did your face wrinkle up a bit? Exactly. It was time to get down to the nitty gritty of who Sparkle Christine was, with Jesus and without him. I don't know about you, but for me I knew it would take borrowing someone else's strength to find out. One thing I have found myself repeatedly sharing with the women I mentor is that true strength is found in our

She Wanted More

weakness. 2 Corinthians 12:9 says, "My grace is sufficient for you, for my power is made perfect in weakness." Therefore, I will boast all the more gladly of my weaknesses, so that the power of Christ may rest upon me. Alright! Who is ready to boast of their weakness now that the scriptures say it is so? Any takers? Not me, that was for sure. Friends, I tell you this, the moment we are tired of being tired, and the longing for change overrides the fear to remain complacent, you may become more in tune with the direction and advice given in this scripture. It was time to work on that healing. The first step was me admitting in all my perfection (or thoughts of it) that there was an issue here— several of them. I had quite a few questions that needed answers. Who was I really? What do I love about myself? If I had to take a good long look at my characteristics, how would the list read? Who was I in Christ, and who am I without God? God finally brought me to the place where it was time to address me and my weaknesses. Up until this point, I became an expert on addressing and pointing out everyone else's weaknesses. Proverbs 29:23 says, "One's pride will bring him low, but he who is lowly (humble) in spirit will obtain honor." Pride increased my pain, but the road to learning humility became one of the hardest battles of my life.

One of the things I love the most about God is the way he lays out the plans for our lives. I like to think he has a sense of humor. After all, if we are made in his image, it makes sense. From the earliest time I can remember we are taught in school and most homes to plan. Plan what career you want to enter, what classes to take in college, what you will make for dinner the entire week, or even something as simple as which route you want to take to get to work, to a friend's house, you name it. On the other end of the spectrum, if you're anything like me, planning was never a focus impressed upon you in your early years. Because it was not originally a focus, I made every area of my life a planning focus. I was going to plan everything out, control it and then implement the actions. I must admit, it exhausted me, made me a dictator to those I

Sparkle Christine

lived with and to myself. Any given day, I could have been asked my short term and/or long-term goal and I would have happily given you the what, who, for and how. Enters in God's plan instead of my own. Here I am moving and shaking in life, blaming everyone else for my issues. There were issues in my marriage that I chose to blame on my husband. Sure, the breakdown of our relationship had some destructive pieces that were far out of my control at times, but it takes two to tango. There were many times I chose to disrespect and disobey the position my husband held as my spouse and leader in life. God showed me time and time again that my pride would only break the strands, not sew them back together. I ignored him. During this time, God moved us to Nashville, by way of a job transfer. Years prior I prayed repeatedly for God to move us there. It did not happen in the time I wanted it to happen, so I gave up. A year after I stopped praying for it, it happened, and fast. Within a span of three weeks, my company transferred me, internally kicking and screaming because I had gotten comfortable. I would miss my family, my church, my community and most importantly I had not planned for it. It was then that I felt God's sense of humor as I reflected on Jeremiah 29:11, "For I know the plans I have for you," declares the Lord, "plans to prosper you and not harm you, plans to give you a hope and a future." Ok God, I am following you. That sounds good, but it was more like, "Ughhh ok God, it wasn't in my new three-year-plan, but let's do this." God was about to humble me in more ways than one. He just decided Nashville was the place to break me down just to build me back up.

Going through a divorce is tough! Going through two by the time you are 32, is a different experience. If I was brutally honest with myself, and at that point I had to be, we should have never gotten married. Our selfish pride prolonged our foreseeable divorce thus inhibiting us from moving on. Again, there were things on his end that could have been done differently, but I am in no way attempting to tell the story to demolish the character of my daughter's father. I decided long before

SHE WANTED MORE

writing this book, that I would only communicate my truth, not intentionally assault anyone during the process. For that reason, I am choosing to primarily address my own shortcomings, weaknesses and sin associated with the marriage. Jesus can and will address any part either one of us played. So, during the incredibly dramatic divorce and the ensuing months, I sat in discontentment, sadness and self-pity. Who am I, and why do I always end up with the short end of any stick? God said, don't look at the external forces or people, and look at yourself. Examine yourself. Matthew 7:3 says, "Why do you look at the speck of sawdust in your brother's eye and pay no attention to the plank in your own eye?" That hurt, but I needed to hear it. Off to therapy I went. There were many years during my youth that I went to therapy. This time was different, it had to be different. I was determined. I was sad. I was tired of being tired. I wanted to be set free.

Therapy was like a gut punch that left you feeling light and airy in the brain. I remember sitting across from the woman, arms crossed, telling her I don't trust easily but I wanted to be better for my kids. She needed to fix me so I could be a better woman and mother. We stared each other down, and by the end of the discovery session, I was dazed wondering what would come next. Oddly enough, she didn't offer much feedback, just asked me so many questions that it left me trying to understand how I had not completely fell apart years before that moment. For several sessions she focused on guiding me through a process of learning who I was. When I arrived at her doorstep, I was an overachieving, overworked, depressed mother. It appeared I had it all together, but, and from many perspectives, I was one red light from a massive meltdown. Numbing out to any emotion that wasn't anger was the first thing I needed to work through. One of the things my therapist shared will resonate with me for the rest of my life. She said that I did the best I could with what I had to deal with, at the time in my life that I developed that skill of numbing out. Translation? My immediate reaction of turning off all emotions was the way I learned to self-protect

Sparkle Christine

early on. Today, my life no longer requiressuch a defense mechanism. I was no longer a victim of circumstance, who needed to numb out. There was a world full of emotion, love and peace just waiting for me to reach out and grab it. Would I be brave enough to step out on faith to obtain it?

Accepting my anger problem sounds like an easy thing to do, especially if you haven't battled it your entire life. It was hard. It was difficult to come to grips with the truth of knowing I was no better than those in my life who had dealt with me harshly. It was difficult understanding that I had issues that I could not solve on my own. When you are stubborn and independent, the last thing you want to accept is needing any form of assistance to grow or change a character trait. I was angry. Angry for how my marriages had not worked out. Angry for being a teen mother who could not experience a different life because of my own poor choices. Angry for growing up in poverty. Angry for being abused. Angry for not being heard. Angry for not knowing who I was, what I liked, what I wanted to do. Angry for feeling trapped. Angry for being in my thirties but feeling like I was years older. I was just plain angry, and I am sure a little bitter too. With the help of my therapist, I was able to give all those things their proper place in my heart and mind. In the past, when I thought about the root causes of my anger, I would get upset all over again. Each situation was addressed and confronted with raw emotion, not anger. I discovered a different effect this time. Initially, I was confused, but then I understood that crossing through the river instead of going around it brought a much more effective result. Healing had begun to rest on my shoulders. I began a lengthy process of allowing myself to feel the pains of life that I shut out so long ago.

Learning the causes of my constant state of anger was the tip of the iceberg. Walking through that process brought me directly to the door of abandonment. Feelings of abandonment left me feeling empty and

She Wanted more

weak. It was as if I lived in a constant state of fear thinking everyone in my life would leave me. I remember the first time I verbally communicated that notion to another person. I was having a discussion with someone about why I would readily give my family money when asked, even to my personal detriment. I would respond and say that I was afraid to say no. I was afraid that if I was not available for them when they needed me, no one would help me when I needed it. Somewhere along the path to this thing called adulthood, I picked up on the idea that love and relationship, any relationship, was one based on exchange – that is, the exchange of actions. In my world, you get what you give. In my fear of abandonment, I would not consider myself or what I could lose in the process of serving someone else's needs. As I think back over friendships, relationships and even parenthood, I clearly see the error in my judgement. Love is not based on exchange of action. Romans 5:8 says, "But God demonstrates his own love for us in this: While we were still sinners, Christ died for us." I didn't have to do anything for God to love me, not one self-depreciating thing. What a relief! He was and is the ultimate example. Why was it so hard for me to see that? Fear and distrust.

The stubborn in-your-face-woman that existed, was drowning in fear. My exterior appearance often radiated strength, might, and just a bit too much grit for the common person. Inside, I was curled up in a fetal position crying out in fear from every area of my life. Imagine the cries of an infant receiving their first set of immunizations. Yes, that's exactly it. Excruciating pain and I wasn't sure until therapy how and when it would end. So, why was this overly confident, steely person so afraid? One word: Pressure. For one thing, I felt the pressure to keep up the tough exterior I built. There is nothing worse than spewing a mouth full of confident crap to your team or peers, while cringing on the inside because you have social anxiety and feel ill anytime you must speak publicly. Did they see me sweat? I sure felt like they did. Somehow, God had given me a career and a lifestyle that I needed to keep going. When

Sparkle Christine

I was at my worst and not walking close to God, I would forget that it was his power that kept my career and life steady, not by my might. During those times, I would feel pressured or anxious. I am in sales. For my friends that are not in the industry, let me tell you something. Sales is a constant goal, and if you aren't careful, it can ruin your life. By ruin, I mean it can sometimes cause you to focus on it in an unhealthy way, especially if your goals are not being met, clients aren't purchasing, or your competitors are posing as a threat against you. A career in sales can be rewarding, but only when you properly prioritize it in your life.

Hear this people; when you are a teen mother, you feel pressured to prove the world wrong. This is true even if no one muttered one word about the teen mother stigma. Anyone relate to me on this? So, the teen parent stigma is that your life will be hard, and your child will follow in your steps. Because of this, I felt pressure to raise this perfect child, get her past the age of 17 to break the generational curse of teen pregnancy, and provide a totally different life than the one she was born into. Not only that, I now had to deal with the stigma of being a twice divorcee. In my mind, I was running on the hamster wheel of fear. Anger, abandonment and fear all lay beneath the surface of a bubbly sales professional. I would go home at the end of my day exhausted from smiling. One of the things I was taught at my first hotel sales position, was that we are on stage. We are paid to sell the dream and experience of travel. Hospitality professionals know how to check their bad day, mood or circumstance at the door. We enter hyped up and ready to sell the dream and we leave that way too. In my world, it was Happy Tuesday every day all day. There were times when I wouldn't make it home before the tears fell. It was no Happy Tuesday for me. It was all going to crumble soon. I like to think of it as crumbling the tower of sand to build a fortress of brick.

Meanwhile in my therapy sessions, I began to learn the benefits of meditation to help with my panic attacks. In the past, I would mask them at work by saying I was going to take a walk to get out of the

SHE WANTED MORE

office. Now, I would walk during brief moments in my day to complete meditation exercises. Focusing on breathing techniques was a tool I could carry alongside my pressure and anxiety to meet the next expectation, whether at work or in my personal life. Managing the anxiety created by my fears was only partially the answer. Through my process of discovery, I learned more about myself. For the first time in my life, I was discovering Sparkle! You know what? I liked what I found. Each day brought a yearning to know more about this woman who was even a mystery to herself. Friends, spending time with yourself is a must. I realized that since childhood, I had not had the opportunity to spend quality time with myself. It felt like weights were dropping off me by the pounds. I appreciated learning about the things in my character that I needed to improve upon; fear, abandonment issues and anger. I even more so enjoyed focusing on what I liked and what I disliked. Have you ever done that? If not, I suggest you write out a goal to do so and get to it. Oh, the time I wasted in learning about other people before I discovered the girl in the mirror!

There was a major shift in my friendships and how I viewed the people in my life. The more time I spent getting to know and love myself, I started seeing others around me much clearer than in the past. I was the person who always had just a few people in her circle. I had believed in small connections. Anything more than that gave me anxiety. How would I split my time between so many people? At the time, I believed that to be true, because I am as authentic as it comes with relationships. The people closest to me can attest to me requiring authentic organic relationships. I began to see that for me to grow into maturity I needed more people in my life. If I only had two or three close connections, how could I gain different perspectives on my character, or parenting, or even relationships with men? Proverbs 11:14 says, "Where there is no guidance the people fall, but in abundance of counselors there is victory." I needed guidance because I was going for my victory. I wasn't going to let a thing like anxiety stop my blessings. I began to branch out

Sparkle Christine

and form relationships. I attended the singles ministry events at church. I connected with a local brunch club and started networking with ladies of sophistication. It was a time that I can look back on with gratitude that I stepped out on faith. Even with my trust issues, I knew God would not fail me. He would not show me that I needed people in my life and then allow me to be hurt. The trick is to be rooted in Him and not people. Getting to understand who I was as a person gave me the opportunity to see my faults and ultimately the faults of all humans. We as people will at some time or another disappoint each other. It wouldn't be discovery if it was all fun and games, right? I not only needed friends to have fun with. I needed friends who loved me enough to say, hey, stop tripping. I needed women in my life who could gently rebuke me and push me towards maturity. Maturity in my walk with God was and will always be key to succeeding at this thing called life. So, I latched on to some wiser women and started digging into more of the things that made me a mess. I am grateful they loved me enough to put up with all my junk and help me unpack it. Get you some friends that will be that for you. It's priceless.

It was then that I really began to want to work on my relationship with my mother. We had gone through so much in our relationship. We coexisted and rarely spoke on any subject that was beneath the surface. Sure, we were able to hang out and do family activities, but it was rare for us to have a heartfelt conversation. As I fought through learning myself, I became curious about her. There were times growing up when people would say that we were similar, and I would laugh or scoff it off. But the more I focused on my own characteristics, needs, weaknesses and strongholds I figured something out. We had so many similarities that it took me by surprise. I now try to envision my mother when she was in her thirties with four children. I could feel the anxiety rising in my throat to think on it. She must have felt all the emotions and feelings I myself have felt at times. She used to say she loved to travel and wanted to do so many things. Oddly enough, I only saw her as my

She Wanted More

mother who held an unhealthy attachment to her husband and sometimes her kids, depending upon the situation. Silly me, I was so selfish in my own desire to be understood, I never tried to understand. Here sat a woman who desperately wanted to be loved and understood. It didn't sound so foreign after all. In fact, I think I could relate to this woman. She sounded vaguely familiar.

It started with a phone call. My mom and I would talk every couple of weeks. I had the foolish notion that all was right in my world and that family would distract me from the new life I had built for myself. That was one of the dumbest thoughts I have ever had. Again, make sure you have some friends to pull you back from the foolishness. This is a prime example of something that I would not have done if I had people counseling me in my life. I digress. I set a goal to be mindful of her. I wanted her to know that I loved her and that I wanted to make up for lost time. I was trying to forgive myself. I knew she didn't hold anything stupid I had done against me. However, this time I would not make this about me. The goal was to make her feel loved and special. The kids and I took a few trips back home to spend time with my mom. I learned how to talk to her while seeking where to understand. You know what happens when people don't feel attacked? Icebergs melt and relationships mend! Today, we enjoy each other and create memories. I love how we can create new memories to erase some of the old ones we don't need to focus on any longer. Who knew unpacking my junk would bring about so much restoration?

Something began to happen on the inside of me. A spark ignited. More and more, I would feel the pulling of an authentic smile. Here is the thing. The problems didn't change. I was still divorcing my husband. I still worked in a demanding industry. I still became a single mother again. Now, the energy was different because I was different. Each day I woke up determined to allow whatever emotion I felt at the time to roll through me and out the door. I no longer operated in the belief that I need to quench or hide the real me. Oddly enough, the real me was a

Sparkle Christine

very emotional, not angry, person. Even better, I was ok with it! You know what happens when you make a conscious decision to just be yourself? You relax for starters. There is also this big internal discovery that moments are just moments. They don't last forever. I don't want to paint this unrealistic picture like I don't still battle some of these things, or that I am not still discovering more about myself with each passing day. What I do want you to understand is that to even get to that point, you must be ready and willing to experience the journey involved. One foot in front of the other, one day at a time. There were days when it was minute by minute. I was curious. I wanted to know my weaknesses, strengths, and everything in between. Let me be clear, when you finally figure these things out, you may relapse over the course of the journey. However, you will have clear indicators of when you are off track. Get back on the wagon and complete the course. The reward will bring you unexplainable joy.

6

Ministry? I Think Not

Ephesians 4: 11-13

"So Christ himself gave the apostles, the prophets, the evangelists, the pastors and the teachers, to equip his people for works of service, so that the body of Christ may be built up until we all reach unity in the faith and in the knowledge of the Son of God and become mature, attaining to the whole measure of the fullness of Christ."

THE WORD MINISTRY GIVES ME A JOLT OF ANXIETY. I am sure that is the reason I ran from it for such a long time, snuffing out the Holy Spirit, like you would a candle. James 3:1 says, "Not many of you should become teachers, my fellow believers, but because you know that we who teach will be judged more strictly." If that didn't discourage the fearful part of me, this next one did. Titus 1:7 says, "Since an overseer manages God's household, he must be blameless-not overbearing, not quick tempered, not given to drunkenness, not violent, not pursuing

Sparkle Christine

dishonest gain." If you read any of the previous chapters, you must know at one time I have been all these things. One of the most challenging things about accepting God's calling on your life, is processing the guilt you feel for not being blameless. I often wondered, why me God? How can I, someone with a past so full of lust and sin, help anyone see your face? God answered. Why not? The process of evolution had to take place to bring me into the arms of grace. The second, third, fourth and fifth chance to love, grow and learn. I am not called to teach because I am blameless. I am called to teach because I am not blameless. Did you catch that?

We all know how the enemy comes to steal and destroy. He has been on this mission to destroy the calling God has on my life since before I was in my mother's womb. When he fails one way, he tries his hand another way. Another reason for my hesitancy to speak my truth and walk into God's call was because of how young I was. I would tell myself things like, "how can I help anyone, and I am this young?" "What can I teach a woman older and wiser than me?" For sure, I was to be laughed out of any room I walked into to share and inspire. During my time in my fellowship in Memphis, I had the opportunity to attend and participate in a women's prayer session. The woman facilitating the gathering approached me and asked if I would share a word, a brief message to inspire the women. I was mortified. I was by all accounts a baby Christian, and all around the church were many women much older by age and by being in the faith. I wanted to run, hide and throw up. I pushed, God pulled, I ran, God seemingly sat on me. I did it. I walked right into the gathering, fell on my face in prayer and shared my thoughts. I spoke on the story of Shadrach, Meshach and Abednego from Daniel 3. It was on blind faith. After the event, I was talking with a sister, and she was telling me how encouraged she was from my message. I ended up telling her about my anxiety from it all, and the narrative that played in my head. She shared, "1 Timothy 4:12, don't let anyone look down on you because you are young, but set an example

SHE WANTED MORE

for the believers in speech, in conduct, in love, in faith and in purity." In this case, I was the one looking down on myself. God can use anyone. Amen for God placing that sister in my path to speak that word from him to me.

I like to overthink and complicate things. The awesome thing about God is that he knows the innermost parts of us. In my opinion, my spiritual dad has a huge sense of humour. I picture him laughing at me when I start to get in my own way and overthink the process. So, there I sat with the knowledge of understanding that God wanted me to step out and do something. Enters in Sparkle and her anxious controlling thoughts. Who else can hear the tunes from a scary movie when the killer is on their way? I was full of anxious questions on how to get from point A to point Z. How do I do this? Who do I tell? When do I start? Where do I go? I wore myself out not trusting the process or walking in faith that God would reveal every necessary step. I spent nearly a decade on the hamster wheel of fear. I admit that even though I am committed to seeing this ministry through, I still do, at times, feel fear to just walk and not look for guardrails. It might not be about ministry; it could be anything else in your life that causes you to pause in doubt. What are your guardrails that you need to drop and just put yourself out there? My biggest guardrail was my codependency on people. What I didn't count on was God using this guardrail to lead me right to him. In my life, people have failed me, and I have failed people. I learned that God will not fail. He led me out of my own Egypt, some of circumstance, and others of my own making.

Let's consider the story of Jonah in the Bible. Jonah fled instead of listening to God. This is what I chose to do early on when God told me to write the book and start the ministry of working with women. I heard what the Lord said, and I did the exact opposite out of fear. I hid from God's presence and went right back into my strongholds that kept me from God's presence. He said, "move" and I did not. My friends, this is what I have learned, when there is work for you to do, it is not always

Sparkle Christine

for you, but for someone else. Selfishly, I was holding someone back from the freedom they so desperately desired. God calmed the sea after the men threw Jonah into the sea. This was a bold statement of his sovereign authority. In one glorious moment, our humanity displayed our weaknesses, and equally as important his strength. If he could do that, why was I so concerned with getting from A to Z? When Jonah arrived in the belly of the fish, the scriptures say he cried out to God from the place of "Sheol". Sheol means place of darkness, cut off from God. Jonah cried out for relief from being cut off from God. I remember feeling that so many times over the past few years. It would be during my times of disobedience to the call. It's a painful feeling, and I knew just like Jonah that I was in sin. It goes on to mention in his prayer of repentance, he said, "those who cling to worthless idols, forsake faithful love." Every time I let go of God's love to search out or do my own thing instead of writing the book and reaching out to women, I ended up in the belly of the fish. He just wanted Jonah to show up to the people of Nineveh. Just like the story, God wanted me to go out into the world to offer a solution, a life jacket. Why should they have to drown just because of my fear, my selfishness?

What did me not giving in to selfishness mean? It meant me seeing God's way as the only way. Hands down, get out of the way Sparkle! I don't know about you, but me getting out of my own way is one of my biggest issues. Anybody else struggle with that? What does your selfishness look like? Let's look at it like this, let's reflect on what the fruitages of the spirit are. (Galatians 5:22, 23). It says nothing about selfishness. If I was to walk with God, I had to emulate him and his way. I would be headed on a one-way trip to disaster if I did not adhere to it. I was not going to end up in the belly of a whale, situation or anything else. Looking at my life, I realized my pattern of giving in to selfish and vain ambition over selfless action. Sure, I may have reached out to others and gave of myself in certain ways. However, there were other times when I knew what to do and went in the opposite direction.

She Wanted more

Experience is our best teacher at times. During my second marriage, there were many things that took place early on that should have made me flee quite frankly. In my own selfishness, I stayed. This was at the expense of my children. I am not proud to say that, but it is what happened. I wanted what I wanted, and how they would feel about it was secondary to my own agenda. I wanted my husband and family, although it was not what was emotionally best for them, or myself for that matter. Giving in to that selfishness cost me and my daughters later. I could loudly hear God screaming for me to get out of my own way.

God made so many things clear after I stopped running. The message was clear. The work he had for me to do was to minimize me and increase HIM. How selfish was I to keep freedom to myself! Now, don't get confused because I may have sounded confident in myself with that statement, and you may have pictured 5'4" me running around with my hand held in the air rushing to victory, but the truth, my friends, is this; when God speaks to me, it's never a loud resounding sound but a quiet truth that makes me feel confident in HIM and HIS ability to direct my path while I utterly trust in him to make me the vessel. What a relief! So, I didn't have to have it all figured out? I did not have to live this perfect life, in this perfect box, trying to look all perfect. Can you sense the freedom? Exactly! God does not want us to live in a box. He wanted me in all my imperfection to be broken, sincere and just humble enough to share my experiences with you. I had it all wrong. Ministry was about me sharing my life and how it all led back to a God of love. It was about me understanding my weaknesses and knowing through mercy and grace I have been forgiven.

During my time in Minnesota, I noticed how women would gravitate towards me. Being an introverted anxious person, that was very unsettling to me then. I wasn't this largely charismatic person who wanted to be the center of attention. It just usually played out that way. I would attend the events at church, and by way of conversation end up

Sparkle Christine

sharing what was on my heart about Christ. Back then, I was what I like to call lukewarm for Jesus. I had knowledge of the Bible and his purposes for my life. I lacked that special connection that kept me focused on my gratitude. I lacked geniuine repentance. Playing church when it was beneficial and living my life when it wasn't was my norm. It was told to me that an anointing was over my life. It had also been told to me that blessings and curses could not come from the same tongue. I never forgot that, and it has stuck with me for over a decade now. How could I be anointed and outrageously outspoken all at the same time? "But God," is all I can say. See, here is the thing, friends. God can have a calling on your life and allow others to see it before you can fully see it for yourself. His revelation for our lives does not alter who we are currently. It just shows our inability to be who we are called to be on our own. The entire mess that I was, and am is not who I am with Christ. As I continued the journey to understanding His will for my life, the physical manifestation of the plan began to take place. 1 John 4:4 says, "You are from God, little children, and you have conquered them, because the One who is in you is greater than the one who is in the world." I will always recognize that greater is he that is in me, than he that is in the world. Without that acknowledgement, blessings and curses would continue to pour from my mouth. That cannot be.

Unofficially, or without me understanding that it was a ministry, I began to reach out to others. I would take in any woman who was in need. While in Minnesota I opened our home up to two different women and their families. The instant I learned of a need, I felt a responsibility to fill it and pour myself out with a home, resources, prayers and whatever else was needed to fill any voids. At times, without so much of a thought to what my husband and child would say. There was a need and we had to come together and meet it. It was in those moments I felt I was walking in my purpose. Then I would hear God whisper ministry and I would quickly dispel the thoughts and shift my attentions elsewhere. He was showing me, opening doors for me to reach out to others and I

She Wanted More

still ignored the call. What would it take to get my attention? Why would I rather control, when and how I served instead of listening to an All-Knowing God? To listen to Him would mean full trust. There would be many more years ahead of me for God to build my faith before I would respond with a, "Here I am, send me."

I was never fully sold on the idea of women being in leadership. It has always been a point of interest to the men I've dated or been married to. How this woman who led others in her professional life could, not believe that women should lead spiritually or have others follow her? It did make for a hearty argument. Before you start to raise your eyebrows, let me explain. Growing up, my mother took us to the Kingdom Hall. Ring a bell? The Kingdom Hall is where the Jehovah's Witnesses fellowship. That's right. I grew up a watchtower carrying, door knocking Jehovah's Witness. Don't all go silent at the same time. If I had to be honest, and I am going to be, it created a solid foundation for my biblical knowledge. Now, I don't agree with many of the principles, perspective of the Bible or other things. I will say that I am grateful for the requirement to study out the scriptures. I learned how to read and study my Bible as a young child. My mother read us the stories of the Bible and prayed with us every night for as long as she attended.

Oddly enough, I was never baptized in the Jehovah's Witnesses church. My mother attended for a few years, and then some things happened, and she left. That is not my story to tell, so that is all there is to that. I digress. By then, I was much older and would attend church with my granny when she visited from Indianapolis. Our family had a church in Hyde Park, in North Memphis, that I began attending. It was a Baptist Church that my aunts and uncles attended. My granny and her family grew up in Hyde Park, so that is and will always be the family church. I was first baptized into the faith there. I was 15 years old at the time. At any rate, my granny and everyone else was happy about it. If any of you are aware of a southern Baptist church, you know it has its own flavor.

Sparkle Christine

The men led everything, and if the women participated, they sang in the choir. Women also would line all the children up to recite their Christmas poems, etc. Looking back, if I were to try and reflect upon a time where I clearly saw women in leadership in the church, I would be hard pressed to see it. Granted, I wasn't attempting to see God's plan for my life at 15. Every experience gave me the narrative of women not leading anything, at home or in the church. This impacted my view of marriage, the home and the calling from God.

From my earliest memories of the church structure, women were not in leadership. We took our direction from the men and adhered to those scriptures that said women should be quiet in the church. This does bring a little side eye when you think about how brazen and aggressive I have had to be as a leader in a sales organization at times. However, I struggled with that when I felt God's call. I still do, then I remember that GREATER IS HE, GREATER IS HE, GREATER IS HE! It has been very difficult for me to grasp the idea that God wants me to share his message with a greater audience. The fact that I am a single woman has made that much more difficult to understand, with my background. When I looked around, the only women spiritual leaders I saw were those whose husbands served in the church. If your husband was a leader, then you were also. I have no husband, so how could I have a ministry? God said, "Fix your eyes on me, not them." Amen. That is what I had to do both then and now. Trusting God is not tested when you are in your comfort zone. Trusting God is practiced when you are not. Answering the call is not one of comfort. I don't believe it is designed to be. Everything I am doing now is something I've never done and that is a faith walk. Total submission to His will and not my own.

I believe our first ministry is our family. Before I could step out, I needed to understand and learn more about serving my family. God has provided many opportunities, and some of my own choosing for me to understand that ministry must start there. It was 17 years ago when I began building my family. I had no clue what I was doing, and if you ask

She Wanted More

my teenager, she might tell you I still don't. Somewhere along the way growth, maturity, and God's love turned my heart of stone into flesh. (Ezekial 36:26). God uses the worst of us to bring glory to his name. I was an unwed teen mother. Many times, I walked in all the spirits that were placed in my life from an early age. The spirit of confusion, the spirit of anger, the spirit of abuse, the spirit of depression all had control of my life at different times. I would walk out of my house after displaying all those qualities to my family and child as if nothing was wrong. No, my friends. Everything was wrong. Outside of the fact that I had some strongholds to break, I was not focusing on my first ministry, my family. It was not until God showed me during my time spent in therapy, addressing those strongholds, did I clearly see what I was doing to them and to myself. I had to repent. Sometimes I would wonder what people would think of me if they knew some of the inner parts of me that struggled with things like that. I know the answer now. I am not ashamed anymore. Even the ugly parts of me helped build my testimony. I am relatable to anyone who struggles with anger, depression and anything else that can cause lack in the family. Who am I today? I am a woman who when not carefully walking in the Spirit, can still struggle with not making my family my first ministry. That is my truth, and the truth of it is, I will never be perfect. But I will be open and honest about what I need to stay on track. I need Jesus. I know who I am in the physical. I am here to speak to who you are in the spiritual.

Quite a few years after my first baptism and the birth of both my daughters, I found myself at another spiritually dead place. I couldn't figure out why. At this point, I knew there was an anointing over my life. I was still stuck somewhere between knowing it and wanting to live my life on my own terms. Life was beating me up and I felt a spiritual tug of war on the inside of me. Sound familiar? During all of this, I started working at a hotel in Memphis. There was a man who worked there, and he invited me to a Bible study at his home. His wife and I became friends and I began studying the Bible with her. I knew the Bible, but I

Sparkle Christine

mean we really studied it. The words that I had studied for many years began to look different, feel different and affect me differently. How could this be? God was changing me. This was all part of his plan. Ultimately, through looking at my life versus the life I was called to, I decided to be baptized again. I recommitted my life and continued my deep study of the scriptures. Does that mean along the way I haven't fallen astray? Absolutely not. Many times, I have taken my own life into my hands by choosing my wants over God's instruction for my life. When I came back, God taught me about grace. I like to think that my fallacies help me to stay grounded. I used to think perfection was what is needed. I was wrong. Honesty, Godly sorrow, and the commitment to get back up after you fall is what's needed. I have failed many people in my life. I have not always been the best parent, friend, lover or advisor. Does that mean that God cannot use me? No, and imperfection does not mean he cannot use you either.

I have made no secret of where I started my life. I boldly walk in every experience that shaped me into the woman I am today. God still chose me. Broken, beaten and lost. He chose me, even though I might not fit the mold of what some may call a leader, motivational speaker or good example for young women. I don't have a seminary degree. I love trap music, Aerosmith, watch Golden Girls and consider myself the biggest introvert (can you believe it!). My qualifications? I am qualified through Christ Jesus. Every experience in my life from infancy led up to the calling God has on my life to walk with others through challenging situations that require a relatable spirit. Today, I accept it. I walk it, and I proclaim a blessing to every woman, man and child that hears God's call on their life to do something, anything that you aren't currently doing to walk through the fire of fear into manifestation. I didn't choose ministry. The ministry of God chose me. What is choosing you right now? Are you running from it? Just for one moment, imagine who can be impacted by your decision to say yes in boldness, instead of no in fear.

Ezekiel 33: 30-33 felt like cold water being splashed in my face. It talks

SHE WANTED MORE

about not understanding the true meaning of God's word until you do what it says. I was ready to do what it said. It was time to hear him and walk in the plan for my life. Are you ready to walk in your plan?

7

Manifesting the Dreemz

WHEN I WAS A KID, I LOVED TO READ BOOKS. Books were my friends who took me away from the reality I so wished wasn't mine. My love for reading returned, but this time with a new discovery. I loved to write! I kept journals over the past few years but was never consistent with it. As I continued to grow in self-love, I would write more and more in my journals. Around this time, I had an epiphany of sorts. Some call it a breakdown, I call it an epiphany. I decided to leave the company I worked for. In many ways I was burned out. For the past few years I worked fifty hours a week building my reputation in the company and in different markets. I had done well for myself by the world's standards. I made Director before I was thirty years old. I had sold eight different hotel brands, and in three different markets. I understand many people

SHE WANTED MORE

work much more than that and for longer, but this is my story to tell. I was tired and depleted of all energies. I was stressed, divorcing again and new to a city I didn't know much about. In therapy, I realized I wasn't happy, and it was time for a much-needed break. I took a different position in the same industry with a company that held a high reputation of being family oriented and rich in culture. I also began a new personal journey. In the past, corporate America was my only focus and goal. I ate, slept and breathed my career. I never stopped to give one thought to doing anything that would be remotely related to making me happy on a personal level.

I took a leap and started a blog for women. I laugh to think of what some of my industry and personal friends thought. There was never a time in my life that I, prim and proper Sparkle, would have ever given the impression that I wanted to write a blog. In the deep recesses of my heart, I knew this was only the beginning to something bigger that God was going to do. He was strategically placing things together to begin building the ministry to reach women battling strongholds. I wasn't' ready to fully expose my vision. While at work, I referred to it as business, all the while knowing it was to be a ministry. The blog was centered on women's empowerment and addressing issues of the heart in a safe space. As I fought through my trials, I always wondered who else might have gone through it. Some experiences are easier to handle if you have a community of women cheering you on to victory. God gave me a vision to create a safe space. I had to give the people what I knew I needed. I needed and still do rely on community. When I mentor women, one of the first questions I ask is who is in their life. Friends, there is a saying that your network determines your net worth. What would you say if I told you that I am here to put a different definition to the word? What if I told you that your net worth is not what you economically contribute to society, but what you contribute to those around you in a different way? Your time, talents and support are the indicators I suggest we start weighing it against. If that is the new

Sparkle Christine

definition, can you see how your network would determine this? Who is breathing life into you? Are you sharing ideas and dreams with friends? Who is cheering you on or pulling you away from the edge of a not so great idea?

1 Corinthians 15:33 says, "Do not be misled: Bad company corrupts good character." Another scripture that references this is Ecclesiastes 4:9-10. It reads, "Two are better than one, because they have a good reward for their toil. For if they fall, one will lift his fellow. But woe to him who is alone when he falls and has not another to lift him up!" Community inspires us all in the fight for growth. My mother is a tough lady when she wants to be. Growing up she would tell me that women could not be friends. I was better off without them. Women were not trustworthy, so put nohope in relationships with them. As I grew into adulthood, I chose to follow that philosophy. Yep, sounded right to me. They were the enemy who would stab you in the back if you got close enough. What a lonely life that belief brought me. Respectfully, the woman before you today must disagree with that viewpoint. I understand my mother's concern for seeing me betrayed in this fallen world where many of us refuse to value friendships and trust. However, I often wondered what life could have looked like for her if someone had created a safe space for her to simply be. With all of this in mind, I sat down to pen the vision God had given me for my introduction to the women that would ultimately join the community of support.

Many years ago, God began to speak to me. Back then, with everything in me I would cry out and ask him why he would allow me to feel so much in my short time on the earth. He would tell me that there was purpose in my pain. I desperately wanted to believe God and I did. I would have visions of me ministering to women all over the world. I was still finding my way, so I would dismiss the visions and tell him that I was the wrong person for the job. When I surrendered to His will for my life and sat to pen the thoughts, an outpouring occurred. The focus had to be on community and grace. When we think about grace, it is typical to

SHE WANTED MORE

think about the grace God shows us first. Then, we move into thinking about the grace we should show others. The grace I wanted us to focus on first, was the grace we needed to show ourselves. Now, if you read the beginning of the book, you can imagine that there were many things in my life I had to forgive myself for. Taking the time to acknowledge the pain we bring ourselves is instrumental in breaking strongholds, generational curses and pushing towards desired change. One of the meanings for the word grace is, courteous goodwill. Let's marinate on that for a second. Courteous goodwill. Typically, that would mean we are extending some sort of goodwill gesture towards another person, right? Imagine the value we are placing on ourselves by sharing some of that goodwill with the one person you will be with for the rest of your life, yourself. Simple, yet so hard for many of us to grasp. I don't know about you, but I could use some courteous goodwill in my life.

Authentic connections and conversations were going to take place and it would start with me. I knew I would have to share more of my story and experiences to create conversations. This is what it was to be about. To create a safe space, I had to operate as though it was already a safe space. The woman I was speaking to would have travelled a long roadseeking change and encouragement. God said we would be daring enough to break down the walls of insecurity. The topicsrevitalized usas we cheered each other through triumphs and trials of many kinds. Throughout my time of therapy, I had developed habits of meditation. I found it very helpful in navigating hectic periods in my life. The tool I found much success in had to be shared with the community. How deflating is it to be motivated, empowered and fired up only to discover that it was a temporary feeling, but you need some permanent solutions. The goal was to include tools for use in our daily life. Meditation has transformed how I view quiet moments in my day. I even find ways to incorporate mediation into my prayer life. I couldn't keep that golden nugget to myself. Simply put, there was a need for Empowerment for Women through Community, Education, Mindfulness

Sparkle Christine

and Grace. With that, Sophisticated Dreemz was born.

I challenged myself with showing the women vulnerability. What is more vulnerable than starting a website and opening yourself up to the internet, fresh off the therapy circuit? It was time to Sparkle and Shine for God's glory, not mine. If vulnerability is what it was going to take, then that was what I was going to do. Minimize me Lord and maximize your might will remain my only prayer. My very first blog still brings tears to my eyes. It was a testimony to how we can trust God to never fail us, to challenge and push us past the limits we unknowingly set for ourselves. I threw myself into writing about topics that gave me a gut punch. Anything that brought me discomfort in sharing was the indicator that I needed to fight through and share it. Leaders, ministers and coaches must understand one thing in order to powerfully walk in the assignment over their lives. The message, situation, circumstance or testimony is not always for them. If we do not fight to obediently deliver what God places on our heart, we could inadvertently cause someone to stumble in their journey. Time and time again, I was shown that delayed obedience to the calling on my life was still disobedience. I was moved to talk about things that we would usually quietly discuss with our besties, or not at all. Push, God said, so I did. I remember blogging about my suicide attempts. The outpouring of support, kind words or similar stories received was unexpected. The awesome thing about God is that if it is something, he wants for us, he will always send confirmation for it. The reaction and calls from those who followed the blog was another faith building opportunity so I would keep reaching. What has happened in your life that built your confidence enough to keep fighting, keep pushing, and stay focused?

Amid blogging, I began to study out coaching, the human mind and behaviors. I learned many things for application. It gave me perspective on things that I found I struggled with. There were also things that I studied that gave me insight on my family. It was then that I began to see a connection between ministry, behaviors and therapy. When I

SHE WANTED MORE

started the journey writing the blog, I also started taking classes to become a life coach. I wanted to not only help others meet their goals, I needed the insight to understand how culture, environment and emotions played into the equation. I was an entire semester into it before I learned something important. Coaching is bringing out the "thing" that is already inside of you. It is done by accountability, encouragement, and consistency. Just maybe, coaching and ministry could go hand in hand. I think back to the times in my life I felt utter desperation to just be understood and encouraged. I wanted a consistent friend, a consistent companion and a consistent will to live. Could I reach those women who wanted the same thing, and help them see Jesus at the same time? "Purpose, purpose, purpose," God said. It is here that I would find healing and purpose. Look at my life. Here was a person who started out life very troubled. God protected and shielded me through it all. I was able to gain experience and build my testimony. What was I to do with it now? What now God? The small whispers I heard from him throughout the years would all make sense one day.

Guess what happened next? I'm blogging, I'm encouraging anyone with a need, I'm even playing with the idea of writing this book and in walks someone whose life looked just like mine did. Cue the tears. It hit me like a ton of bricks. God said, this is it. Manifestation. Do my work. She started sharing with me and for a while I was speechless. Esther 4:14 comes to mind. "For if you remain silent at this time, relief and deliverance for the Jews will arise from another place, but you and your father's family will perish. And who knows but that you have come to your royal position for such a time as this?" The abuse, the pain, the numbness, the emptiness, the self-hatred, the suicide attempts, the teen pregnancy, the drug abuse, my God the story. God gave me all that history to impact someone else. I came from all of that for such a time as this. How could I not step up and into manifestation? It was my full circle moment. All I could do was thank God for showing it to me, and then get to work. By work, I mean prayer and through God speaking life

Sparkle Christine

into that woman. God gave me the testimony and he did the rest. Practical's came from my coaching training. There are practical's involved with healing that one must not ignore. There are practical's involved with ministering in the lives of others. Some were new to me and others were things I have used for most of my life without knowing what they were.

In the process of healing I hit a bump in the road. I'm writing the book, the blog, ministering to the women who seek me out and some I seek out. I hit a rough patch in my parenting and in my job. Overall, distractions started taking place. I took a few months to process it all before I could pick the pen back up or even the phone to talk to people. One of the most important things to remember when you are walking into manifestation, any calling or thing you must do, remember that you will be tested. Don't waiver in your faith and keep that same energy, sis. Keep that same energy no matter what is being thrown your way. That is when your tribe must step in, pull you back in, and helpkeep you focused. In my case, I pulled away from my tribe, and reverted to the introverted Sparkle that I was in the past. This worked well for me until I would get that strong knock on the door. You know the one I'm talking about? The one where you think it's the police even though you are an uptight law-abiding citizen. Yep, that's right. It was my friends, sometimes alone and sometimes in a group ready to sit on my couch and pull me out of my distraction, depression, or whatever it was at the time. Every situation or circumstance is an opportunity to grow. My take a way from that was to pour out, which means you must continually be fed or refilled. Who is in your life? Where are you being poured into as you pour out? Where are my mothers out there? This applies to you too. As women, we pour out and provide and give every inch of ourselves to our children. For us to be fresh and accommodating for them, we must keep our cup full first. That is where that word 'selfcare' came from. I needed to create boundaries and make sure I was being fed as I poured out.

She Wanted more

Let's talk about this bump in the road more. It happened to me and it will inevitably happen to you once or twice if you're not careful. How could the newly inspired, mindful coach fall into the sunken place? Here is how. She, and by she, I mean me, stopped opening her toolbox and reverted to the self-narratives that held her back for so long. I began struggling in my work, and I started to believe I wasn't worthy. Lies. I began having conflict with my teenager and I started to believe I was struggling because I became a mother very young. Lies. I began questioning spiritual principles I had been taught and I started to think maybe I was not supposed to minister if *I* was confused. Lies. There were allthese things that contributed to my inability to hear God tell me to keep moving in my purpose. Distractions happen in our lives. It is how we overcome them that matter. How are you currently working through the distractions in your life? What is your pattern? Can you see your pattern? I no longer wanted to be like the yoyo I played with as a child. I would get all the way down to the end of my test, and then I'd be quickly yanked backbydistraction. Pattern identified? Check. Game plan in place? Check. Tribe or friendships to keep me accountable. Check. You know what happens to the distractions after that? That's right. Check Mate.

Now that I experienced my full circle moment, my bump in the road, and I was fired up to walk in my purpose, like many of us, I had to keep it moving. Here I am God, send me! God said do the coaching and build the ministry. I have had all sorts of questions from the people in my life. Do you plan to start a fellowship? Will you talk to your church about this? What next? Will you remain in Corporate America? Let's slow down for a second. My answer is and will always be, Holy Spirit lead me. I desperately want to reach and serve those who are in the process or have broken strongholds offtheir lives and want to explore what is next. I desperately want to serve Christ in His kingdom across the world. Christ has women all over the world that need to hear my testimony, and yours too. We must use DREEMZ to get there. What is DREEMZ? It

Sparkle Christine

is going to help us cross barriers to reach, teach and encourage those who are ready for next level breakthroughs. It is **Daring** to confront self-narratives, **Revitalizing** through introspection, **Engaging** in authentic discussions, **Edifying** activities to connect mind and body, **Mindfulness** that leads to peace and prayer with **Zero** apprehension to stir up inner passions.

In the process of writing this book, I can tell you without hesitation that I have experienced every emotion I have inside of me. I was fearful for starters. Here I am, with all my faults writing this book. The first thing the negative part of me said was, who is going to read it and why would they care? I don't care if I am talking to the one person who bought the book. That one person may be the one God had me write it for so, Amen! I have all but bared my soul to step out and say, God loves you and he sent me in the shape of my broken and bruised life to share that with you. This has been the ending to a lengthy process, and I can finally say the little girl can rest. She has been set free. She no longer hides in fear of being found out. What are you looking to be released from? For many years, I have walked in a deep sadness for the way my life began. Today, I am renewed in spirit with the knowledge that there was purpose in my pain. Hallelujah! Thank you, Father, for the experience! I no longer regret any part of my life that created who I am today. I am fearfully and wonderfully made, and so are you. I share my life in hopes that it will help you find joy in wherever your life is today. If it's not joy you are in search of, then maybe it is peace from your past that haunts you. I encourage you to pray for a set of fresh eyes to see what God has for you in that experience. Psalm 139:14 says, "I praise you because I am fearfully and wonderfully made; your works are wonderful, I know that full well." 34 years later, I know that, I accept that, and I embrace it. To God be the Glory, Amen.

8

Journaling Through Dreemz

HAVE YOU EVER STOPPED TO THINK, WHAT IF I AM GOOD ENOUGH? What if I can break through barriers inside of me to invoke change? Can my life be different? Real strength comes from asking questions and then being determined to work through the steps to answer them. Often it is our self-narratives that determine what we do, where we go, how we feel and how we challenge ourselves. My friends, it is time to change that and unpack your stuff. While working to develop my faith to step into the call on my life, I asked myself questions to help me understand what was holding me back, and what I needed to identify before starting my journey. I wanted to share them with you. Take some time either after each chapter, or at your leisure to work through the questions below. Self-evaluation is important to understand where you are and where you want to go. It is my prayer that they will lead you to deeper insights with where you should start your journey or understand the necessary steps to get to the next phase

Sparkle Christine

in breaking the walls of fear, and ultimately living the life God designed for you.

Take some time to write down one-word emotions, thoughts or feelings associated with how you feel about yourself, how you've ever felt about yourself and how you would like to feel about yourself. Divide it into three columns.

_____
_____
_____
_____
_____
_____
_____

Over the course of time, have those thoughts or feelings caused hesitancy in how you made decisions? How?

_____
_____
_____
_____
_____
_____

Take a moment to think through how anxiety or depression may have

SHE WANTED MORE

caused you to navigate situations. If you had to cull it down to one integral moment, can you pinpoint the external circumstance that may have shifted how you began to view your abilities?

_____
_____
_____
_____
_____
_____

Imagine for a moment what could happen if you broke your walls of insecurity to work towards a different outcome for your life? What would that look like?

_____
_____
_____
_____
_____
_____

What are your patterns? What situations do you find yourself in repeatedly?

_____
_____
_____
_____
_____
_____

Sparkle Christine

What makes you feel safe?

_____
_____
_____
_____
_____
_____

What are you longing for?

_____
_____
_____
_____
_____
_____

How have you tried to dig your way out of what you are struggling with?

_____
_____
_____
_____
_____
_____

Who is in your life to help with accountability?

SHE WANTED MORE

_____
_____
_____
_____
_____
_____

Journaling can open the door to healing. May you be blessed with revelation as you begin your journey to your Second Act!

ABOUT THE AUTHOR

Sparkle has been a lifelong writer who began with poems and spoken word. She discovered her passion for writing as a child, and watched it reignite in her thirties. She is an avid reader, and favors famed authors, John Grisham, Joyce Meyers, John Eckhardt and J.D. Robb. Sparkle has a vision of ministering to women across the world as she shares her testimony. Her humble beginnings ultimately led her to Christ. In 2015, she fully accepted God's call on her life and began seeking a deeper relationship with the Creator. In 2019, she founded Sophisticated Dreemz, a faith-based organization designed to coach, empower and lead women into spiritual, emotional and physical freedom.

Sparkle has two children. She lives in Nashville, TN and enjoys wine tastings, running, watching Golden Girl reruns and traveling with her children. Sparkle has a heart for global missions and serving the materially poor. She currently volunteers with the non-profit organization, Hope Worldwide, and serves as the Nashville, TN chapter Treasurer. She proudly represents the Memphis District Order of the Eastern Star, Prince Hall Affiliated, an organization rooted in serving the community. For more information, visit her on the web below.

SHE WANTED MORE

She wanted more...

www.sophisticateddreemz.com

Acknowledgments

I dedicate this book to my daughters. When I look at you both, I am reminded of grace and God's love. In a world that was so dark, he gave me two bright stars. Tiana, you are my firstborn and we grew up together. I am eternally grateful for the gift that is you. You were God's first kiss upon my forehead to show me his love. Madison, or my dear Maddy, you have the inner joy I always wanted. Continue to brighten lives through your loving spirit. You bring joy into my heart, and you are a valued treasure to me. Thank you both for being patient with me as I learned to be your mother. Thank you for your effortless love. I am beyond humbled that God chose me to be the vessel for your lives. May you grow up to love him as your King.

A special thanks to Nick Journey. I believe God allowed our paths to cross for many reasons, some still unknown and a few revealed. Whatever the reason, I am eternally grateful. Thank you for speaking life during a drought, believing in my vision even without fully knowing much about me, and for answering God's call so you could ultimately be a light for me and so many other women coming behind you. My prayer is that God places a special blessing on your life. Your sister in Christ, Sparkle Christine.

www.ingramcontent.com/pod-product-compliance
Lightning Source LLC
LaVergne TN
LVHW011215080426
835508LV00007B/798